PN 54 .A2 B56
Blocker, H. Gene.
The metaphysics of absurdity

WITHDRAWN

THE METAPHYSICS OF ABSURDITY

H. Gene Blocker
Ohio University

RITTER LIBRARY
BALDWIN-WALLACE COLLEGE

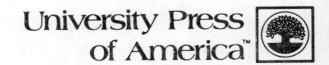
University Press
of America™

Copyright © 1979 by

University Press of America, Inc.™

4710 Auth Place, S.E., Washington D.C. 20023

All rights reserved

Printed in the United States of America

ISBN: 0-8191-0712-3

Library of Congress Catalog Card Number: 78-78399

TABLE OF CONTENTS

PREFACE

This book explores the metaphysical foundations of Absurdist literature and is intended as a general introduction to the philosophy _of_ and the philosophy _in_ the literature of Camus, Sartre, Ionesco and Beckett.

I would like to thank all my students in the experimental Philosophy of Absurdist Literature course at Ohio University who helped me in formulating the major ideas contained in the book. I am also deeply indebted to the American Council of Learned Societies for a 1975 Grant-in-Aid which enabled me to complete my research on the metaphysical presuppositions of Absurdist literature. Finally, a special word of thanks to Lisa Bibbee and Sondra Choto for their excellent and painstaking work in preparing the manuscript for publication.

CHAPTER 1: INTRODUCTION

On several occasions, Ionesco has said of his work,

Two fundamental states of consciousness are at
the root of all my plays . . ., those of
evanescence on the one hand, and heaviness on
the other, of emptiness and of an overabundance
of presence; of the real transparency of the
world, and of its opaqueness; of light and of
heavy shadows.[1]

The aim of this book is quite simply to explain that
statement, especially the paradox of heaviness and
lightness as interpretations of and responses to
absurdity.

In Absurdist literature "absurdity" is a technical
term referring to the divorce of thought from reality,
or, as it is variously expressed, the split of word and
object, meaning and reality, consciousness and the world.
It is, in short, the perceived distance between man as
the source of meaning and intelligence and an independent and thoroughly distinct reality. The problem which
these writers set themselves is to describe as faithfully
as possible what that object is like when it has become
stripped of human meaning. And, as indicated in the
passage above, the description most frequently offered
is that the object alternates between extreme heaviness
and excessive lightness.

Not all absurdist writers emphasize both in such
a balanced equation, some, like Sartre and Camus,
stressing heaviness, others, such as Beckett, emphasi-
zing lightness. Earlier accounts of absurdity tend
toward the heavy side of the equation, later accounts,
toward the light side. The heavy characterization
also tends to be a statement of the problem of absurdity, while lightness is more often an attempt to
formulate a solution. Still, why these two seemingly
contradictory characterizations, and how are they
related to one another?

The answer I am going to suggest is admittedly
somewhat surprising, viz., that the literary problem
of absurdity is basically a metaphysical problem of
being, that the lightness/heaviness distinction is the
perceived correlate of the metaphysical distinction
of being as essence and being as existence, being in
the sense of what a thing is and being in the sense simply
that it is; on the one hand, the "is" of predication,

as in "A unicorn is a mythical beast" and, on the other
hand, the "is" of existence, as in "There is no unicorn."
As a preliminary definition, we may say that "existence"
refers to the object as it is in itself, quite apart
from any human interest in it, while "essence" is our
interpretation of that object. The central concern of
absurdist writers is the metaphysical distancing of word
and object, thought and reality, essence and existence.

In ordinary experience the two are naively joined
together, or, more accurately, are simply not distinguished. This failure to differentiate the two is what
makes for the ordinary experience of a meaningful world,
in which my concepts, concerns are projected on to the
world, successfully adhering to that world with no sense
of separation. The world then appears familiar to me and
I read into it and find within it my own projected concern
and conceptual biases. But when, under various circumstances, I see meaning as mine and the world as other than
my own, the union dissolves and the two split apart--mean-
ing on one side and an alien world on the other. A meaningful world, in short, is a synthesis of essence and
existence, while a meaningless or absurd world is the prod
uct of their separation.

We can now begin to appreciate the heavy characterization of the object without meaning. Shorn of human
significance the object becomes an alien, inhuman, brute,
recalcitrant, mere thing, indifferent to my will and
thus dense, heavy, etc. Metaphysically this corresponds
to the idea of being as existence, that is, an independent reality as it is in itself removed from all human
contact. Take away the human interpretation or essence fr
an object and all that is left is bare existence, and
that is heavy.

But there is another important conception of being
in Western metaphysics and it is this second conception
which explains the alternating lightness of the meaningless object. Being is also understood in terms of essence
what a thing is, its identifiable kind, or semantic
category in which we place the object. Stripped of meaning or essence, objects are just there, brute, bullying,
real existence with no admixture of human interpretation. But stripped of meaning these same things are also
nothing. What are they, that is, what do we call them,
what meaning do we attach to them? By definition, nothing
Hence, they are, in this sense, nothing; they have existen
in the metaphysically technical sense of reality without
meaning, but they have no being or essence. They are there
but they don't exist for us. Hence, their overt heaviness

2

dissolves into an empty, hollow unreality. What is all-
too-real one moment suddenly dissolves into dizzying emptiness. Hence the surrealist tension in absurdist writing
between the oppressive heaviness of the super-real and the
alternating dreamlike quality of empty phantoms.

Metaphysically, we may say that meaningful objects
in the ordinary world of intelligible experience have
both essence and existence. That is, we interpret individual existing objects as belonging to definite conceptual categories, and this is what gives the world
its meaningful shape. Objects in our world do not exist
as bare particulars, but only as objects of a definite
kind--that is, as a tree, as a chair, or as a person.
Being is for us always being-as. This defines the
full sense of being, including both essence and existence,
though a partial sense of being occurs whenever either of
this pair is absent. In a weak sense, therefore, there
are objects like Tom Sawyer, which have a meaningful
essence but no existence. Objects shorn of human meaning,
on the other hand, have existence but no essence; that
is, they have being in the sense of existence, but they
have no being in the sense of essence. In that case
there occur the two related experiences of absurdity, the
first toward a kind of soulless materialism, full of
brute, unthinking, blind matter; the second toward a kind
of mystical Void empty of any meaningful content. The
first is the presence of existence, the second is the
absence of essence. In this sense the two opposed states
are surprisingly complimentary and compatible and even
require one another. They are indeed like two sides of
the same coin.

In arguing a metaphysical interpretation of absurdist
fiction, I don't want to suggest that absurdist literature,
or any literature, for that matter can be equated with
philosophy in any and all respects. Fictional literature
and philosophy are clearly distinct forms of writing, the
most pronounced difference being the portrayal of concrete
individuals in a specific setting in literature as
contrasted with the abstract conceptual framework of
philosophical writing. What I am urging is a relationship
between these two forms of writing.

But what exactly is that relationship? Can a
philosophical idea be expressed in a literary form, and
if so, how is that possible? It has become fashionable
since Croce's identification of expression and intuition
to assert the complete inseparability of form and content
in literature. Indeed this has become a rallying cry of

3

literary formalists and purists for years. Since what
you say always depends on how you say it, it is impossib
to express the exact same content in more than one liter
form, and certainly it is not possible in two such profoundly different forms of writing as systematic philoso
and fiction. In this sense, clearly, novels and plays
are as "untranslatable" as Eliot thought poetry was. Bu
this must not be so narrowly understood as to prevent ou
identifying in a general way literary themes and subject
matter. Otherwise we should be totally unable to expres
even in a rough way, what representational art works are
about. A sensible middle ground, avoiding this extreme
while remaining true to the spirit of those who urge the
inseparability of form and content, would be to argue th
while the _precise_ content cannot be expressed independen
ly of some particular linguistic format, the _general_ cla
into which that particular content falls, along with
members of a shared family of related contents, _can_ be
independently articulated.[2] In this sense a novel, a
political speech, a father's advise to his daughter, and
a play might all express the same theme, though each in
its own way and each with something unique to say within
this broad area. In this sense philosophical ideas _can_
be expressed in works of fiction.

     How then, _are_ philosophical concerns expressed in
Absurdist literature? If we follow Arthur Danto's[3]
definition of philosophy as a concern for the "space"
or relation between thought and reality, we see the
absurdist interest in the divorce or separation of thoug
and reality as _fundamentally_ philosophical. This is
supported by the fact that many of these European writer
are extremely concerned with philosophical issues,
having read and written widely on philosophical matters.
Jorges Borges includes in _A Personal Anthology_ a piece
of philosophical prose, "A New Refutation of Time," in
which he discusses most of the major figures in modern
philosophy, including Kant, Hume and Bergson. Camus
has written a cogent refutation of both Kierkegaard and
Husserl as a way of defining his own position; Ionesco
has written similarly comparing his position to that of
Heidegger; while Beckett has disucssed for many years hi
preoccupation with 19th century pessimists, such as
Schopenhauer and Leopardi, and ancient philosophers, suc
as St. Augustine and the Stoic, Diogenes of Abdurite.
Beckett's first published work was, significantly, a
poem about Descartes' meditations on time. And of cours
Sartre's connection with philosophy is well known, if
admittedly special. The point is that these writers,
perhaps more than their American counterparts, see their

4

own work in a philosophical light. They regard philosophy as the primary means of stating the broad cultural concerns of the age, and they see themselves as addressing these broadly philosophical issues. Obviously this has as much to do with differences in philosophy east and west of the Atlantic (and the English Channel) as it does with differences in styles of fiction.

Several additional factors are responsible for the pronounced philosophical orientation of this particular group of writers. Since Schopenhauer the idea that systematic philosophy deals with things indirectly through generalities and abstract concepts has been seen by many as a limitation, not an advantage. Thus the idea that art deals with the same issues concretely and directly has come to be seen by many artists and writers since the last century as a better way of doing philosophy. As Ionesco remarks,

> Because the artist apprehends reality directly, he is a true philosopher. And it is from the range, the depth and the sharpness of his truly philosophical vision his greatness springs.[4]

Camus writes in a similar vien,

> People can think only in images. If you want to be a philosopher, write novels.[5]

> A novel is never anything but a philosophy expressed in images. And in a good novel the philosophy has disappeared into the images.[6]

As we will see, it is on precisely this basis that Camus criticizes Sartre's Nausea for being too abstract, for a content too divorced from concrete images.

Also, most of these writers see themselves in direct relation to the 20th century philosophical movement known as Phenomenology, in which philosophical themes are often explored by analyzing structures of human experience (for example, in Being and Time Heidegger explores the philosophical question of being by analyzing the structure of free-floating anxiety). As we will see shortly, while themes of existence and nonexistence can be felt and experienced, they cannot be conceptually articulated and linguistically developed. Given the philosophical orientation of phenomenology, it seems only natural therefore to suppose that the best way to write about the divorce of thought and reality would be through the eyes

5

and ears of some concrete fictional character in a novel
or play who is actually experiencing that divorce, such
as the protagonist in Murphy or Roquentin in Nausea.

Finally, a careful reading of the nonfiction works
of these writers reveals such a profound interest in
philosophical theory that one must begin to seriously
question the widespread but simplistic notion of artists
and writers as emotionally sensitive creatures who prefe
to leave the theorizing to the theorists. As we will
see, the absurdist writers are knowledgeable philosophic
ally and are capable of making penetrating philosophical
points in a logical, as well as a literary format.

Nonetheless, the most important philosophical
connection is simply the profoundly philosophical nature
of the central theme underlying absurdist writing -- the
separation of thought and reality.

Nor is this relationship between literature and
philosophy an accident or quirk of recent history.
Despite the "ancient quarrel between poetry and
philosophy" which Plato first observed, the basic proble
underlying absurdity, the separation of thought and
reality, is an old and perennial problem in Western
philosophical thought. It dominates Plato's concern
to find a relation between the sensible particulars and
the Ideas, Aristotle's insistence that the two coexist
in a form-matter synthesis, the old and the modern
problem of scepticism, and various problems of dualism,
such as the mind-body problem, which we find in Descarte
Locke and Kant. Nor is this underlying problem alien
to art and theories of art. Romanticism is primarily th
attempt to bridge the gulf which developed in the 18th
century between a mechanistic conception of reality and
human sensibility. This Romantic bridge is based on the
idealist belief that human thought is actively creative,
and attempts to expand that idea to cover an artistic
creative thought remaking the world aesthetically.
Romanticism, likewise, founders on the realist insistenc
that this is only wishful thinking with no correspondenc
to an independent reality. Some of the absurdist writer
such as Camus and the early Beckett, write directly out
of this Romantic point of view. The world is cold and
ugly, and so humans have remade that world more in their
own image and more to their own liking. The main
difference between the Romantic and the Absurdist point
of view in this regard is the half-hearted optimism of
the Romantic that this creative enterprise of remaking
the world is a process of discovering a new truth about

the world, as contrasted with the thoroughly pessimistic
outlook of his Absurdist counterpart that such an enterprise, however creative, just shows all the more clearly
the unbridgeable gap between man and the world. According
to Herbert Marcuse, the awareness of the gap between
thought and reality defines all art up to, though
significantly excluding our present "one-dimensionality."
In its break with traditional art, modern popular culture
abandons that "two-dimensional" sense, which is essential
to art, of distance between reality and our interpretations of reality. More generally, aesthetic consciousness
has traditionally been characterized since the 18th century
as requiring a self-reflective "distance" or subjective
"detachment" from the objective world. All of which
indicates that the problem of the separation of thought
and reality is hardly new, either to philosophy or to
literature.

The problem of absurdity, then, we want to understand
as part of a much broader metaphysical issue over the
separation of essential being from existential reality.
The world stripped of human meaning is a dense, heavy
world of sheer existence, but is is also a world stripped
of essential meaning, and in that sense it is empty,
evanescent and light. Because of the prevalence of
materialist thought in our culture over the past several
hundred years, the image of real existence stripped of
all human interpretation as something heavy, dense and
indifferent to human purpose is a reasonably familiar
one. A classic statement of this heavy materialist side
of the problem outside the existentialist-absurdist framework is Bertrand Russell's "A Free Man's Worship".

> Brief and powerless is Man's life; on him and
> all his race the slow, sure doom falls pitiless
> and dark. Blind to good and evil, reckless of
> destruction, omnipotent matter rolls on its
> relentless way; for Man condemned to-day to
> lose his dearest, to-morrow himself to pass
> through the gate of darkness, it remains
> only to cherish, ere yet the blow falls, the
> lofty thoughts that ennoble his little day;. . .
> proudly defiant of the irrestible forces that
> tolerate, for a moment, his knowledge and his
> condemnation, to sustain alone, a weary but
> unyielding Atlas, the world that his own ideals
> have fashioned despite the trampling march of
> unconscious power.[7]

What is not generally recognized, certainly not by Russell,
is the metaphysical compatibility of materialistic heaviness and mystical lightness. Indeed, as two sides of the
same coin, neither can be understood completely without

7

the other.

Because of the prevalence of materialistic thought
in recent times, we are far less familiar with the light
side of absurdity. At first glance it may seem odd to
call the semantic category in which we classify objects
a kind or sense of being. It may even seem preposterous
that what we call a thing can alter the object in any
way, or, especially, affect its being. Call it what
you like, if it is, it is! We don't create objects when
we create names for them; neither do objects disappear
because we don't have a name for them. Nonetheless, the
fact remains that it is impossible for us to think of
or describe an individual object without first determinir
what kind of thing it is. Where there is no word for
something, we simply don't notice it, though of course
it might exist nonetheless unbeknownst to us. As an
illustration of this, consider how much you can remember
of your life before you learned to speak. So far as we
know, objects don't exist without essence.

Essence is therefore an integral part of our notion
of being, and indeed until fairly recently, essence was
the dominant conception of being. In order to understand
this aspect of absurdity, then, we need to clarify the
notion of being as essence. And the best way to do that
is a brief excursion into the history of this remarkable
idea.

The story begins somewhat awkwardly and naively with
Parmenides. Parmenides simply identifies being with what
can be thought, that is, with essence and meaning. This
of course implies that only those things which are
intelligible or rational can be, and this raises an
enormous problem. Many things we come across everyday
cannot be reduced to a rational, intelligible order. Wha
are we to say about these things which exist but which
do not meet Parmenides' criterion of being as that which
is intelligible, meaningful and thinkable? Parmenides
says these things only seem to be. Even if we perceive
something, such as change, and can talk about it, as we
can, for example, about things which don't exist, but
can't consistently, logically think them, then such
"things" are not really, but only seem to be. Thus,
radically unique individual existence, change, nonbeing
which can't be rationally thought have no being but only
a seeming. And this seeming has no connection whatever
with being. There are simply these two "ways" of talking
 -- the way of being and truth and the way of seeming
and ignorance. Since the way of seeming includes all of
common sense, everyday perception, and science, Parmenide

8

position is an extremely unhapppy one. Even to speak of
a seeming requires some link, however tenuous, with real
being. An appearance must be the appearance of something
which is not itself an appearance but something real.
And this has been the basic problem over appearance and
reality, existence and essence ever since -- to find how
to relate the two.

If you identify reality with essential being, as
Parmenides does, you must show how real essence is related
to the appearance of individual existence. If you identify
reality with existential being, as modern materialism does,
you must show how this reality is related at least to its
mental appearance and verbal expression -- hence, the
mind-body problem in Descartes and the problem over real
and nominal essence in Hobbes and Locke. In either case,
the problem is how to relate the two. But unlike modern
materialism, Parmenides identified being with essence,
equating existence with mere appearance. He left it to
his successors, Plato and Aristotle, to establish some
relationship between the two.

Plato adopted Parmenides' logical criterion of being,
but tried to overcome the gap between being and seeming,
essence and existence by relating the two in terms of
"similiarity", "approximation," and "participation."
This grants a limited reality to existence (seeming), but
only through its relationship to essence (reality). That
is, something was real only because and to the extent
that it participated in real, essential being, which Plato
called the "Ideas." Like Parmenides, real being was
defined in terms of essential thought. The objects of
rational thought were real; what you think about when you
think correctly about justice, right triangles, piety and
the like obey the laws of thought, such as the law of
contradiction, and so are by definition real. Their
existential exemplifications in the physical, spatio-
temporal world break these laws of thought through
imperfection and change, and so are not truly real. In
so far as we think of such existents in terms of their
ideal counterparts and in so far as they exist because of
these ideal counterparts, they have a limited reality,
rolling about, as Plato described it, between being and
nonbeing. Thus Plato does provide some sort of relation
between essence and existence. But, as Plato himself
seems to admit in Parmenides, it is not a very clear
relationship, and, as Aristotle pointed out, is not much
of a link to begin with.

If the Ideas, or Essences could exist apart from

existing sense particulars, then the entire material world
was gratuitous. The particulars required the universals,
but the universals did not require the particulars, and
indeed, could not, by definition, be in any way touched
or affected by the particulars. And if explanations were
always about Ideas, then the Ideas were equally gratuitous
for explaining the particulars. This left them remote
and disconnected, and so the problem of relating the two
realms of essence and existence continued. Aristotle
tried to develop a more intimate relationship in which
the material existent and the ideal essence were synthesized into the particular, existing objects we find in
ordinary experience, trees, men, etc. Real being, then,
is the synthesis of formal essence and material existence.
As Ross says of Aristotle,

> An individual must have both being and character;
> without matter it could not have being, but with-
> out form it could not have character. And being
> and character are inseparable from one another;
> . . . form and matter exist only in union and
> are separable only in thought.[8]

But although Aristotle put the two together, each remained as unchanged as in Parmenides and Plato and therefore as
incompatible. Like oil mixed with water, the essence-
existence mix soon separated, first in Aristotle's own
philosophical development and then, more so, in those
philosophers who followed Aristotle.

Ironically, in trying to locate essence in material
existence and make sense particulars the center of reality,
Aristotle nonetheless gravitates towards the essentialism
of Plato. Why? Because essence is all that can be known,
thought or spoken of anything. We remain convinced,
instinctively, that there is something else, variously
called matter, existence, substratum, which thoughts are
about and essences are of, but we can't say or think what
it is, for as soon as we do, what we say becomes an
essence! This is what later became known in the Latin
tradition as the essence/existence problem and which comes
through the history of philosophy as the Idealism-Realism
debate.

In modern logical parlance, existence cannot be an
attribute or predicate, not can it be defined. The
difference between a real object and an imaginary one is
a big one, of course, but it cannot be conceptually though
or verbally articulated. Whatever you can say about a
real person could be said about an imaginary person.
It is on this basis that we tell lies and construct storie
Nor can we conceptualize or articulate the difference

10

between a truly described individual and all the other individuals to whom this description also happens to apply. I am, for example, an individual person. But I am not the only individual person. "Individual person" is the name for a large class of entities of which I am only one. How can I characterize my individuality? I am a man rather than a woman, thin rather than fat, a father and a son, and so on. Each of these qualifications narrows down who I am. But clearly no matter how many qualifying descriptions I tack on to this list, I am still left with the name of a class of many possible entities, not the unique one which I am. Existence can't be put into words or thoughts, in short, not into essence.

Yet we can't ignore existence either, as Parmenides tried to do. We know there is a real world existing independently of human consciousness, but we can only describe it in human generalities. Since all we know or can say about existence is essence, existence becomes a gratuitous, superfluous notion, and this is what leads eventually to Idealism, the view that the only things we have any knowledge of are the thoughts of thinking subjects, thus agreeing with Plato that being is essence but internalizing Plato's essences and converting them into subjective phenomena. This is Berkeley's position, for example, that since we have no knowledge concerning an underlying material substrate, we ought to ignore it. This puts the Realist in the odd position of Dr. Johnson who reportedly went out and kicked a stone to refute Berkeley, i.e., a stubborn but inarticulate insistence that there is a reality out there, but with nothing to say about it. Realists also admit the comprehensible world of meaning, or essence, that is, understood reality, as a semantic or psychological reality and so usually end up with the kind of irreconcilable dualism with which it all started in Parmenides, though now existence is real and essence is appearance, the reverse of Parmenides. Locke and Kant, for example, insist on the existence of a reality completely transcending conceptual understanding, accepting at the same time all the difficulties consequent upon such a notion, difficulties which spring in every case from the complete separation of thought (essence) and reality (existence). How, for example, do we know, in the case of Locke, that our ideas are caused by real external beings, and how do we know that our ideas of primary qualities resemble their external causes? Or, in the case of Kant, how do we know that a particular bit of sensible reality has been correctly classified by the concepts of the understanding? As both Kant and Locke acknowledge, there is simply nothing to say about

11

this independent reality except that it just is. Beyond
that we can only classify it in terms of meaningful
essence. Even the idea of the being and nonbeing of an
entity, beyond the stubborn, gut-level insistence that
it just is, is absorbed in essence. To say that X is
is to say that X is an A, where A is a meaningful concep
category or essence, such as "a tree." Similarly, to sa
X does not exist is to say that X no longer belongs to
cateogry A but has begun to be included in categroy B
(it is no longer classifiable as a tree, for example, bu
now falls under the concept of a log). On the level of
articulate thought, then, the being of an entity is tied
up with its comprehensible essence, though in the gut-
level, irrational sense that is "just is," existence
continues to be the ultimate object of thought, transcen
ing any humanly comprehensible essence.

But if there is nothing to say about a totally
independent reality or existence, how can there by a
theory of reality or existence? Strictly speaking, ther
can't, although there can be a voiced concern with
problems which have a direct bearing on existence -- God
creation of the world out of nothing, the idea of life
after death, the unique individuality of the person or
human soul, and other post-Greek, i.e., Christian themes
Thus the contemporary resurgence of existence over essen
begins, with Kierkegaard, as a religious objection to
abstract philosophical thought. Because existence is
inarticulate, the revolt against essence is a revolt
against philosophy -- indeed a revolt against all ration
thought. As Gilson says, "the reaction of existence
against essence is bound to become a reaction of existen
against philosophy."[9] This is also why the best existentialists have been the absurdist writers of fiction wh
seem to agree that while existence cannot be logically
articulated, it can be artistically evoked.

In the modern period, as we have seen, the ancient
reality/appearance character of the essence/existence
split is reversed. While Plato held that essence was
real and material existence was merely an appearance,
modern thought on the whole tends to hold that material
existence is real (though unknowable) and essence is
"all in the mind." An intermediary position was held in
the medieval period which claimed that essences were ide
in the mind of God, thus enjoying a relatively independe
status from men's minds where they have been firmly lodg
since Descartes. Most philosophers after Aristotle can,
therefore, be classified as either Realists or Idealists
Realists tend toward a sharp dualism between meaningful
being (essence) and existence, which is independent of

12

meaning and human consciousness. There is an independent
reality (existence) which we interpret to ourselves (as
essence), but there is no comprehensible link between the
two. Because of the lack of any such meaningful link,
Idealists drop the idea of an independent reality and,
like Parmenides, equate meaningful essence with being.

This age-old debate between the realists and the
idealists, then, comes down to this. Either a thing is
conceptually meaningful or it is not. For the idealist
this is simply the distinction between being and nonbeing. If something is conceptually meaningful, then it
is something and has being; if it is not conceptually meaningful, then it is nothing and has no being. For the
realist, on the other hand, that which is conceptually
meaningless includes not only nothing, or nonbeing, but an
uninterpreted underlying reality which ultimately transcends
human thought, a reality which we try to understand but
which we never completely succeed in reducing to terms of
human thought. Thus, leaving aside for the moment
the ontologically nil category of nonbeing, the realists
admit two ontological categories--reality (or existence)
and meaningful being (or essence), whereas the idealists
allow only one, meaningful being (or essence). Hence the
clash of essence and existence only occurs within realism
and does not appear within idealism.

In the chapters to come we will see how Husserl and
Heidegger (at least in Being and Time) fit into the
broadly idealist category, while Sartre, Camus and the
other Absurdists fall into the realist camp. In fact,
any statement of absurdity as the separation of thought
and reality presupposes the duality of thought and an
independent reality which we have defined as Realism.
For Heidegger and Husserl, on the other hand, there is
no such contrast between meaningful being and reality,
but only that between meaning, which is being, and non-
meaning which is nothing. Hence they understand being
exclusively in terms of essence. Either we have an
understandable something or we have nothing. There is
no sense of an independently existing, transcendent but
unknowable reality "out there", prior to understanding,
which we find in Sartre, Camus and Ionesco, with which are
contrasted both essential, meaningful being and nothing.
It is precisely in criticizing Husserl's "idealism" that
Sartre and Camus reintroduce the Realist position as a
way of defining the gap between thought and existence.

Unfortunately, the full sense of being, as a synthesis
of essence and existence, gets lost in this separation of essence and existence, a separation which is
experienced as absurdity. The being of an object is the
meaning or essence which resides in and belongs to

13

that existing object; it cannot be a mere idea in someone's head set off against a totally incomprehensible
independent reality. The problem of being is precisely
how to relate essence and existence, while the problem
of absurdity is just the experience of their separation.

This central dilemma is nowhere more apparent than
in Aristotle's Metaphysics. On the one hand Aristotle
believes that the world is composed of individual entiti
These may be supersensible, such as God, the intelligenc
or sensible, but they are nonetheless individual particulars. But when Aristotle asks in what intelligible
sense these things are, he is led into the realm of what
is statable, thinkable, and thus into meaningful essence
rather than individual existence. Thus the beings
Aristotle is interested in are existing individuals, but
the being of these beings is essential being, just as
in Plato.

Metaphysics has always been a puzzling book since
it appears to contain two quite different accounts of
metaphysics. According to Jaeger and others, there is
an earlier view which is basically Platonic.[10] In
this sense metaphysics is the science of supersensible
entities, such as God and the intelligences which Aristo
thought controlled the planetary movements. On this
interpretation, physics would study sensible particulars
and metaphysics would study supersensible particulars.
This is the view of metaphysics as a kind of theology.
in Book Z Aristotle asks a new and entirely different
question, "What is meant by the being of sensible things
what is it to be an individual thing?" This is not, as
in the earlier concern, an extension of physics into a
supersensible realm, but arises directly out of speculation about ordinary physical objects. As Randall puts it

> The aim of every science can be stated as the
> attempt to answer the question, What is it to
> be a certain kind of thing?...Now generalizing, we
> can drop off the distinctive kind, and ask merely,
> What is it to be any kind of thing, any subject
> matter whatsoever?...[And the answer is] "To be"
> anything means "to be something which can be
> stated in discourse." It means to be some-
> thing of which we can ask the question, "what
> is it?" ti esti? and get the answer,

14

"it is thus and so" -- of which we can state
"what is is", its _ti esti_.[11]

To be is therefore to be a thing of an identifiable
kind. The central question, therefore, is, What must
any entity have in order to be and to be known, that is,
what are the criteria for our judging that so and so is
and is an object of knowledge? These questions clearly
indicate a concern with the question of being (the
being of beings) which Heidegger wrongly claims had
already been forgotten a generation before Aristotle.[12]

   Aristotle's answer in Z is that to be is to be the
object of knowledge and discourse, something answering
to the question "what is it?" a _what_ which it retains
through a series of natural changes and a what into which
it develops. But of course the answer to such a question
is always a concept or essence, such as "an oak", or "a
man." The question of existence is taken for granted;
assuming there _are_ oak trees, what is it to _be_ an oak
tree, that is, some definite kind of thing; what is the
being of such things? Or, to put it still another way,
What is responsible for that thing being what it is,
namely an oak tree or a man? Thus, the _cause_ of being
is essence. As Ross points out, "the general tendency
of Z . . . is to carry Aristotle away from his earlier
doctrine that the sensible individual is 'primary
substance,' to one which identifies primary substance
with pure form (essence) and with that alone."[13] As a
realist Aristotle postulates a material world of existence
whose being is nevertheless _understood_ by us in terms of
definable essence.

   There is, consequently, a persistent and problematic
ambiguity which haunts Aristotle's discussion of being
which is never satisfactorily resolved. On the one hand
reality consists of concrete, existent individuals; on
the other hand, reality is composed of general essences,
just as in Plato. If we ask, pointing to Socrates, what
is it, we can answer either with the proper noun, Socrates,
or with the common noun, a man. The first is individual,
the second general. This appears in Z as the ambiguity
between substance as the individual (existence) and
substance as a knowable and identifiable kind (essence).
In _Metaphysics_ Aristotle considers the following problem.
What is Socrates? What makes him be what he is? Socrates
is a man, his essence is human nature. Without this he
would not be Socrates, but a tree or an insect. But
this human nature is also Callias' essence. If their
essential being is the same, what differentiates them?
Only their matter, Aristotle proposes, only the fact

15

that the same essential form or essence appears in two
different bits of matter. As Aristotle puts it,
Callias and Socrates are "different in virtue of their
matter..., but the same in form."[14] But this won't
explain how we know they are different and can tell
them apart, since matter is totally incomprehensible.
Throughout Aristotle insists that matter is altogether
unthinkable. If it were thinkable, he reasons, it would
be an essence and then there would have to be something
else nonessential for this essence to inhere in. For a
realist there must always be an uninterpreted reality
transcending human thought and essential meaning, but
whatever a realist chooses to contrast with essence,
whether it be existence, matter, sensation, space or
time, it will have to be something unknowable, and this
will always create problems. Thus we see Aristotle in
Z struggling for the first time with the problem we
now know as the essence/existence problem. For Aristotl
the problem is that his theory implies that we can't
know individuals, which we obviously can. As Ross says,
"Individuals are indefinable; if they have an essence
it is at least indefinable."[15]

     More generally, assuming that real being is compose
of particular individuals, we can go on to ask what
makes them individual, what is responsible for their
individuality. Thus we can analyse the individuality of
individuals, in the same sense as Aristotle asks about
the being of beings. In creating a science of being
Aristotle was not content merely listing all the existing individuals in the world; he wanted an account of
what it is about these individuals which qualifies them
for this description as existing entities. As Ross
notes, "Aristotle is not content to leave it at that...;
he strives to find the substantial element in individual substances."[16] "Individual substances" are concrete
particular existing individuals, while "the substantial
element in individual substances" is being in the sense
of general essence. In terms of the logical distinction between meaning as the denotation and meaning as
the connotation of a term, we can say that the denotation of "substance" or "a being" is simply all those
discrete particular individuals which make up the world,
that is, all the dogs, trees, sunflowers, and so on;
while the connotation of the term is the theoretical
account or definition or essence of what makes a substance a substance, a being a being--a definition, in
short, of its substantiality or being. But since this
is all we can rationally understand about being, the
distinction between a being and the being of that being
is far from clarified. We can feel the distinction in

16

our bones, but we can't say what it is.

Various candidates are proposed in Z to answer the question of the being of an individual, and most are rejected because they do not provide an account of why this individual is the particular individual it is. The Platonic Idea won't do since it is not individual and cannot exist on its own. Nor is matter sufficiently individual and separate. The most satisfying answer in Z is essence since this does provide an answer to what makes what would otherwise be a heap of undifferentiated matter into a single, unified thing of an identifiable kind. Essence in this sense is obviously more than a conceptual or semantic category ("man," or "horse"); it is also the internal principle which organizes the many parts of a horse, say, into a horse. In fact the main difference between ancient essentialism (Parmenides, Plato and Aristotle) and modern essentialism (Idealism) is that the ancients saw essences as objective realities, while modern essentialists see them subjectively as psychological or semantical categories which exist only "in the mind." If we ask what is responsible for the being of a particular entity, the answer is its essence, that is what makes it what it is. But this does not mean that the object simply is the essence; the essence is still the essence of the object, and it is to make clear this distinction that Aristotle proposes a second formula, that substance is a synthesis of form (essence) and matter (existence). The object is essence and matter, though the essence alone explains why it is what it is. All that we can understand, articulate and explain about this individual thing and why it is is contained in its definable essence; the ultimate material elements are completely unthinkable and indefinable. Why does Aristotle retain an undefinable, unknowable term in his account of being? Like Locke and Kant much later, it is simply to maintain a realist position that reality transcends conceptual meaning or essence.

In so far as Aristotle stresses essence as the intelligible being of a thing, his account is very much like Plato's view that being is what can be known, understood, defined. In so far as Aristotle insists that this essence cannot exist apart from a material embodiment, he retains a realist posture, though a very unstable one. Like most realist positions, Aristotle's existence/essence, matter/form duality is constantly on the verge of collapsing into an idealist monism of essence, that is, into Platonism, due to the sheer unintelligibility and hence gratuity of material existence.

17

Since existence is gratuitous, and since dualism is not as tidy as monism, the drift has always been since Aristotle toward essentialism in which being is understood as intelligible, meaningful being. There may be something else of which this understood being is an understanding, but since it cannot in any way be defined or thought or spoken, it is questionable whether it should be introduced at all. Thus when Sartre asserts that existence precedes essence he is attempting to overturn two thousand years of philosophical thought which has held steadfast to the notion that because of intelligibility, essence precedes existence.

Aristotle has introduced two conceptions of being which have been in competition ever since, being as essence and being as existence. He also insists that these two conceptions of being must be combined, although it is not very clear how. Aristotle was the first philosopher to raise the central question about being and, in my view, he was basically right in his answer to it. At first it seems odd to say that what makes an individual be the individual it is is its definable essence, that is, the meaningful concept under which we classify it. Surely, what we call something doesn't make it exist or cease to exist. But however ironic or paradoxical, when examined closely, we see that this is the case. Consider the life story of an oak tree. At some point a flower appears on an oak tree, is fertilized, the ovary then expands, the acorn drops off, sprouts, grows into a sapling, then a tree, which is eventually cut down, and becomes a rafter in a tavern. Notice how many questions relating to the existence and nonexistence of the tree depend on our conceptual categories, that is, on essence. How many existing individuals make up the story, for example? It depends entirely on the system of classification employed. The English "flower," "seed," "sapling," "tree," "log," "rafter" classificatory scheme dictates that there are six objects. But clearly there are other ways of breaking up the continual growth process into as many or as few categories as we like. How many distinct colors are there in the color spectrum? As many as you like. And so with the tree. Imagine a language in which "hunk-of-wood" covered both living and dead wood, that is, including what we designate "tree," "log," and "rafter". In this language the number of objects involved in the above story would only be four: flower, seed, sapling and hunk-of-wood.

Consider now another question, at what point does an object begin to exist within this story, and when does it cease to exist? Again, it clearly depends on what we're talking about, that is, it depends on the category in

18

which we place the item. In the hunk-of-wood language
there is no point in the story when the tree ceases to
exist and a log begins to exist; in our imaginary language the occasion on which the tree is felled and prepared
for milling is simply an episode within the lifespan of
a single entity which remains what it is throughout, viz.,
a hunk-of-wood. And it would remain a hunk-of-wood until
something happened to it which removed it from that category and placed it into some other category, for example,
when it is ground into pulp and made into newspaper. In
short, things can be said to exist or cease to exist, to
come into existence or pass out of existence only as
objects of a certain kind, or essence. Similarly when we
consider what changes are of the radical sort which make
the object stop being and which are of the relatively
minor sort which merely form an episode within its life
history, we see that it depends in every case on the category in which we place the object. If the concept in
question is "tree," then cutting it down and removing
all the branches is a radical change which makes it cease
to exist. Of course, "it" does not cease to exist entirely;
like the magician's rabbit which simply disappears, it
merely ceases to exist after that point as a tree. "It",
or another "it" which takes its place, continues to exist,
though this time as a log. The irony is that there is no
existence or nonexistence of distinct individual entities
without humanly assigned concepts or essences which define
the kind of entity in question. There are no distinct individuals without lines to demarcate one from the other,
and there are no lines of demarcation without human concepts. Individual existence turns on its general essence;
being is being-as. An individual object is neither an
existent entity nor a conceptual interpretation of that
entity but the synthesis of the two, the interpretation
of that entity as a thing of a certain kind. You can't
have existence without essence. As Roquentin observes
in Nausea, when words and concepts cease to "attach" themselves to objects, objects cease to exist as discrete
particulars and begin to dissolve into one another in a
way which Roquentin describes as a kind of "fog." From
this point of view we can understand the mystic claims,
which have impressed both Ionesco and Beckett, that the
world is empty, not in the sense that a new house is
empty but in the sense that without human concepts there
are no distinct individual entities which come into being
at some point and later pass out of existence. There is
a rainbow, but there are no discrete colors in it.

   Apart from mystical notions of the void, there is a
long debate in philosophy over the meaning of statements

19

about nonexistent entities. Parmenides felt that since
the objects of thought could only be, nonbeing could not
be an object of thought. Plato tried to find room for
meaningful statements about nonexistent entities by
analysing nonexistence in terms of difference. To say tha
Theaetetus is not tall is not to say something about a
nonexistent giant Theaetetus, but only to say that the
category into which Theaetetus falls is a different one
from that into which tall persons fall. This is like our
tree-log example; to say the tree no longer exists is
not to speculate about something called The Void, or
Emptiness which suddenly swallowed up the tree, but only
that what had been previously classified as "tree" is
now classified under a different label, "log." Just as
being, in the sense of essence, is defined in terms of
the semantical category into which an entity falls, so
nonbeing is defined in terms of the semantical category
into which it fails to fall. This notion of negation has
been revived in the present century in the work of Heidegg
and Sartre. Heidegger's Das Nichts nichet nicht means
that nothingness is not an objective power or force or
thing in the world, but arises only out of a peculiarly
human way of perceiving the world. We expect something,
and when that expectation is disappointed, we speak of
absence, of something not being there. In Sartre's famous
example, we look in at a cafe and see that Peter's not
there. There is no Nothing, no Void inside the cafe;
indeed there are plenty of people, tables and chairs
there. There is only a failed expectation, that is,
there is nonexistence only relative to a human concept or
essence. We can feel existence in our own case and worry
over our potential nonexistence on a gut-level; we can
even try to evoke this feeling in art or fiction. But
we cannot think either of them logically. Existence and
nonexistence appear as independent entities, that is,
only on a rudimentary, instinctive level, as in the situations typically explored in existentialist novels, e.g.,
a man about to be shot. On the level of articulate though
both existence and nonexistence are defined in terms of
essence. Philosophically, essence precedes existence.

It is only within this ironic tension between essence
and existence that the important question of being arises,
where both the object and the what of the object are perceived as inseparably related, where existence and essence
are distinguished but operate in a mutually dependent way,
in the inseparable union of X-understood-as-A. Only on
an abstract level of words and concepts do the two appear
distinct and separable. So, for example, it seems plausib

20

for Descartes to inquire first <u>whether</u> something exists
and then <u>what</u> that something is, as though we could determine whether something exists before we know what kind of
thing to look for. As an experiment, look around the room
and determine the number of medium sized bliks in the
room. Of course you can't do it until you know what a
blik is. If we define a blik, for example, as any manu-
factured article with three or more separately made parts,
you will then have no difficulty counting the bliks,
that is, all the chairs, tables, and so on in the room.

Similarly, Ross and Gilson in their criticisms of
Aristotle likewise assume a sharp and clear division between existence and essence, as though we could consider
the two issues in isolation from one another. They criticize Aristotle for confusing two quite distinct senses of
being. Gilson, for example, writes, "What is true is that
essences are and that individuals exist."[17] Therefore,
according to Gilson, Aristotle,

> bungled the whole question. The primary mistake
> of Aristotle, as well as of his followers, was to
> use the verb "to be" in a single meaning, whereas
> it actually has two. If it means that a thing is,
> then individuals alone are, and forms are not; if
> it means <u>what</u> a thing is, then forms alone are
> and individuals are not.[18]

But this sounds a little too neat. It is not clear that
there are two distinct senses of being. The two are not
separable but mutually dependent sides of the same coin.
Aristotle's intuition that being only arises out of the
<u>synthesis</u> of the two is therefore more fundamentally cor-
rect than his critics' charge that he <u>confuses</u> the two.

Nonetheless, historically, the synthesis which made
the question of being and our experience of the world
meaningful became unstuck, and the question of being de-
generated either into an unclarified notion of bare existence (Locke and Kant, for example), or, on the other hand,
into an idealist identification of being with conceptual categories, or as the most encompassing and therefore
most abstract conceptual category. That is, the notion of
being degenerates historically either into the idea of
existence without essence or into that of essence without
existence. Since there is nothing to say about the former,
except that it "just is," metaphysical speculation gravitates toward essentialism. Since in the modern period
essences are internalized and psychologized into mental
ideas and conceptual semantic categories of classification,

essentialism drifts further in the modern period into some
form of transcendental logic (Kant) or subjective idealism
(Berkeley). Metaphysics, in other words, becomes a science
of concepts, and a science of reality only where minds and
their concepts are said, by idealists, to be the only
reality. Absurdity is the <u>experience</u> of this degeneration of the question of being.

For Aristotle the question of being is, what is it
which makes something be, what is it in virtue of which we
say it is, what do we <u>mean</u> when we say it is. The answer
to which, as we have seen, is the significant identification of an existing entity <u>as</u> a thing of a meaningful,
essential kind, a category which reveals that entity to us
as a thing which we can know and understand. This is a
philosophical articulation of the common sense merging
of existence and essence, in which there is no separation
of the thing from what we call it. But due to the early
Platonic doctrine in <u>Metaphysics</u> (metaphysics as theology,
the study of immaterial beings), the question of being very
early split into two subspecies, metaphysics as theology
and metaphysics as being qua being, the <u>being of</u> beings,
which we find in Z. Throughout later Greek, Roman and
Arabic philosophy the central problem of metaphysics was
reconciling these two conceptions of metaphysics. Eventually the second notion, being qua being, collapsed into
a notion of being as the broadest and thereby the most
empty class concept. "Plant" is a broader class than "tree"
and "living thing" is still broader, and so "being" is the
broadest of all, including <u>everything</u> within it. But the
more items a concept contains, the less specific is its
meaning; thus "being" as the class of everything is as
emptied of concrete meaning as "thing," and just as unin-
teresting. But whether as theology or as the largest
class concept, what we <u>mean</u> by "being," that is, the question of being, gets lost.

In the modern period the essences which Plato and
Aristotle took to be real, nonmental constituents of the
world become mental concepts by which human beings classify things in the world in thought and language. Metaphysics now becomes a science of concepts, a "transcendental" logic in Kant, exploring the form of our thought
rather than the substance of the world. In the post-
Kantians this psychologistic transformation of essences
continues. By dropping the notion of the <u>ding an sich</u> as
gratuitous, and reifying and objectifying the concepts which
Kant had studied transcendentally, <u>as</u> concepts, essentiali

22

comes to rest finally in idealism. Within the idealist
framework, reality is thought, so the science of concepts
becomes the metaphysics of a mental reality. Although
idealists objectify mind as the only reality, essences
remain psychologized as the subjective mental states of
this mind reality. For Kant the notion of the thing-in-itself, though severly truncated, kept the science of concepts on the thought side of the realist divide of thought
and reality, within what Kant called the "transcendental"
or "critical" philosophy. By dropping the ding an sich as
gratuitous, the postkantians, Fichte, Schelling, and Hegel
objectify logic. In so far as Phenomenologists, like
Husserl, reject the notion of a nonphenomenal, transcendent
reality, they continue, though perhaps unwittingly, the
traditon of idealist metaphysics.

Hegel, for example, reinterprets Kant's notion of
Reason as the critique of conceptual paradoxes of Understanding as positively, objectively founding a new science
of a dynamic reality. Where Kant saw Reason exposing contradictions, Hegel sees Reason as discovering contradictions;
where Kant saw Reason's job to undo contradictions (anti-
nomies), Hegel sees Reason as discovering objective
syntheses which objectively overcome real contradictions.
This is a bizarre twist on the ancient tendency to read
criteria of thought into reality. Instead of the traditional dictum we saw in Parmenides, "if there are no
thought contradictions, there are no real contradictions,"
Hegel says, "since there are thought contradictions, there
must be real contradictions."

But in this intricate, meandering historical Odyssey
the question of being gets lost. The question of being, the
being of beings, presupposes a synthesis of essence in
existence. But this synthesis, which is clearly reflected
in the common sense refusal to differentiate concept and
object and which Aristotle sought to rationally defend in
Metaphysics, is left far behind in the course of metaphysical
speculation. Practically from the outset word and
object, thought and reality, essence and existence have become irreconcilably estranged from one another.

Absurdity is the experience of these metaphysical problems of splitting word and object, essence and existence,
though as we will see in the chapters to come, these metaphysical themes will surface in absurdist literature in a
variety of different ways. First in the characterization
of the ordinarily meaningful world of naive experience as
the union or cohesion of thought and reality, concept

23

and object. Then, in the description of the loss of mea
as the breakdown of that union and the consequent separation or divorce of two distinct terms--the human and th
nonhuman, along with the insistence, especially in Camus
that the problem of absurdity depends on the recognitior
of an independent, alien reality. For both Sartre and
Camus, to experience absurdity one must be a realist--wi
out an independent reality to which thought can fail to
correspond there is no disappointment and no problem. Ab
surdity, therefore, can never appear within the framewor
of idealism. Then, in Sartre and Ionesco, there is a
penetrating description of the experience of a world wit
out humanly assigned meanings, first as a dense, brute,
bullying, nonhuman matter proliferating, choking and
crowding us out, and then, as a transparent, light, empt
world devoid of meaningful human content. And finally,
some of Ionesco's work and most of Beckett's, there is a
reappraisal of the light side of absurdity as a positive
solution, transcending the two term gap which creates th
problem.

     Part of the absurdist concern is with the divorce c
word and object, language and reality, as a function of
more general thought-object split. Consequently languag
is a key concern of these writers. Ordinarily the conve
tionality of our own language is transparent to us, a
matter of blind Habit, as Beckett calls it. Words successfully attach themselves to objects, and the world is
linguistically packaged and hence intelligible. In the
experience of absurdity, on the other hand, words will n
longer project themselves outward nor attach themselves
to objects, and so become opaque entities in their own
right. The result is the frustration of a useless langu
no longer performing its proper function, as in Sartre's
Nausea and Ionesco's The Bald Soprano, but resulting als
in a feeling of wonder in the presence of a world sudden
stripped of its familiar film of language and looking
brand-new, which is a frequent theme of Ionesco. As we
will see, a great deal of absurdist writing is concerned
to demonstrate and even to bring about that alienation c
language from the world. Since language is the medium c
fiction, this is important both in terms of the form and
also the content of absurdist writing, the first concern
being to expose (make opaque) the ordinary naive attachment of word to object in everyday speech. This results
in a powerful dramatic technique of placing ordinary,
mundane conversations in bizarre situations which disloc
and distance the language. In Amédée, for example, an
ordinary middle-class couple are worried what the neighb

will think about a giant corpse which threatens to grow
beyond the bounds of their small apartment. Secondly, following this exposure of the opaqueness of language, there is
the resulting difficulty in describing the "naked World",
as Sartre calls it, which has been stripped of its familiar
garb of identifying labels. And, finally, just as objects
without words are alien, so are words without objects.
Hence a frequent theme in absurdist literature is the
threatening aspect of language once it has been dislodged
from its proper function in a worldly habitate, a wild,
hostile force completely out of control. In The Lesson
words not only can but actually do kill!

However dominant these metaphysical themes in absurdist writing, it is important to emphasize that these themes
are integrated into related social and psychological
themes. In Ionesco, for example, heaviness appears as
social conformity (A Stroll in the Air and Jack) and human
brutality (The Killer, Amédée and The Lesson), as well as
metaphysical alienation. The relationship between these
themes is actually much closer; metaphysical themes are
generally expressed in social and psychological terms. As
a work of fiction the metaphysical themes are conveyed, not
in abstract concepts, which would result in an odd sort of
fiction, but in what Eliot called their "objective correlative" of social and psychological reality. As Camus
said, the philosophical ideas must be expressed in images.
On the level of images, for example, a man rents an apartment and then proceeds to be buried in tons of his own
furniture (The New Tenant), but this is clearly meant to
be understood metaphysically as an analogue for the sense
of mechanical proliferation of oppressive matter (dense,
heavy existence divorced from essence), a favorite theme of
Ionesco (e.g., The Chairs, Amédée). In Beckett's Endgame,
to take another example, a young man named Clov debates
leaving his master, Hamm, and their stifling abode for an
emptied world outside, which on another level, conveys the
possibility of choosing the positive, liberating lightness
of absurdity over its suffocating heaviness.

Also, as we will see, these themes are not always pre-
sented in their purest or most extreme form. In Nausea
there is a progressive dissolution of word and object,
beginning with the simple failure to identify a single
object (the stone, or the tree root) in a context of still
identifiable objects (the beach, the park), continuing to an
awareness that all distinctions demarcating objects are dissolving into a kind of fog, and coming to rest finally in an
almost Buddhist sense of total emptiness. At first, that is,
the object without meaning retains a kind of thingly identity.

It is recognized generally, say as a piece of furniture, b
not more specifically as a chair. But this is only the
thin edge of the wedge. As Kant showed, even the identification of it as an object involves the projection and
objectification of linguistic concepts on to the world. A
these more fundamental concepts become dislodged, the sens
of emptiness spreads until it becomes total, as toward the
end of Beckett's Murphy. There are degrees of absurdity,
and the experience and portrayal of absurdity can appear
at any point along this continuum.

There are also clearly marked differences in the absu
ist treatment of emptiness or lightness. At first lightness is a disturbing sense of being lost, cut loose from a
familiar world and is therefore experienced negatively
as a disquieting loss of orientation or direction. Later,
however, as in the radiant city in The Killer, A Stroll in
the Air, the end of Amédée, and Endgame, this same emptiness is embraced as a solution transcending the dualistic
problem of the word-object separation.

Despite these complications, the unravelling of which
will occupy the bulk of the following chapters, the thesis
I will maintain throughout is that the underlying theme of
the works of all these writers is the metaphysical separa-
ation of thought and reality, essence and existence.

NOTES

1. Eugene Ionesco, "Point of Departure," Leonard C.
Pronko, trans., in Theatre Arts, June 1958.

2. Gene Blocker, "The Meaning of a Poem," The Britis
Journal of Aesthetics, v. 10, 1970.

3. Arthur Danto, "The Transfiguration of the Commonplace," The Journal of Aesthetics and Art Criticism, v.33,
1974, p. 141.

4. Ionesco, in Martin Esslin, The Theatre of the
Absurd (Harmondsworth, England: Penguin Books, 1968),
p. 130.

5. Albert Camus, Notebooks 1935-42, Philip Thody,
trans. (New York: Alfred A. Knopf, 1969), p. 10.

6. Camus, "On Jean-Paul Sartre's La Nausee," in Lyrical and Critical Essays, Philip Thody, ed., Ellen Conroy Kennedy, trans. (New York: Alfred A. Knopf, 1969), p. 199, from a review in Alger-Republicain, October 20, 1938.

7. Bertrand Russell, "A Free Man's Worship," from Mysticism and Logic, reprinted in Selected Papers of Bertrand Russell (New York: Random House (Modern Library), 1927), pp. 14-15.

8. W.D. Ross, Aristotle's Metaphysics, vol. 1 (Oxford: Clarendon Press, 1958), p. cxv.

9. Etienne Gilson, Being and Some Philosophers (Toronto: Pontifical Institute of Medieval Studies, 1952), p. 142.

10. Werner Jaeger, Aristotle, Richard Robinson, trans. (London: Oxford University Press, 1948).

11. John Herman Randall, Aristotle (New York: Columbia University Press, 1960), pp. 110-111.

12. Takatura Ando, Metaphysics (The Hague: Martinus Nijhoff, 1963).

13. Ross, op. cit., p. ci.

14. Aristotle, Metaphysics, 1034a5, in The Basic Works of Aristotle, Richard McKeon, ed. (New York: Random House, 1941).

15. Ross, op. cit., p. cxv.

16. Ibid., pp. xcii-xciii.

17. Gilson, op. cit., p. 50.

18. Ibid., p. 49.

CHAPTER TWO: CAMUS

For our purposes Camus represents the classic definition of absurdity in its clearest, simplest terms. We
will therefore begin with Camus and examine the other absurdists by way of contrast with Camus, looking not only
for similarities and differences, but ways in which
Camus' initial concept is subsequently developed, enlarged
and refined. As such Camus will assume a position in this
book as the most straightforward and least sophisticated
account of absurdity. This strategy is somewhat unfor-
tunate in that it does not fairly represent Camus' broad
perspective and balanced point of view, and we must make
it clear at the outset that and how it does not.

First of all, absurdity for Camus is only the beginning, not the end of wisdom. One begins with absurdity
because this is the problem to be solved. Camus is therefore critical of writers like Sartre who, in Camus' view,
appear to give absurdity the last word.

Accepting the absurdity of everything around us
is one step, a necessary experience: it should
not become a dead end. It arouses a revolt that
can become fruitful. An analysis of the idea
of revolt could help us to discover ideas capable
of restoring a relative meaning to existence,
although a meaning that would always be in danger.[1]

And in the Notebooks he writes, "One must not cut oneself
off from the world...My whole effort...must be to make
contact again...with nature first of all."[2]

Secondly, even in the beginning recognition of the
problem, absurdity cannot be properly analysed in purely
negative terms. Absurdity for Camus is always a tragic
response, and, as he argues in "On the Future of Tragedy,"
tragedy is born of the irreconcilable opposition between an
unacceptable reality and an unlimited hope. It can exist,
therefore, only within a tension of both positive and
negative elements of experience.

People have thus been able to write that tragedy
swings between the two poles of extreme nihilism
and unlimited hope. For me, nothing is more true.[3]

As he makes more explicit in The Myth of Sisyphus, the

tragedy of absurdity depends equally on both factors, both the human expectation and the world's refusal to meet that expectation. Without the former there clearly could be no _failure_ or _refusal_ of the world to honor human deman upon it and thus no problem or tragedy. Thus the tragedy absurdity ironically requires a sense of the great and elevating side of life to balance its grim opposite. Moreover, if that positive sense of life is not to be dismissed as a completely groundless, irrational dream, it must have some basis in reality. In his early critique of Sartre's _Nausea_ Camus not only argues, as mentioned earlier, a lack of balance between the philosophical conte and the imagist form of the novel ("a lack of balance between the ideas in the work and the images that express them"[4]). He also condemns Sartre's lack of balance, essential to tragedy, between the wretchedness and the beauty of life. Without this balance, he argues, there simply is no tragedy. Sartre's failure in _Nausea_, Camus charges, is "the failure...to believe that life is tragic because it is wretched. Life can be magnificent and overwhelming--that is its whole tragedy."[5]

And finally, there are indications, here and there, in Camus' writing, which we will examine more closely toward the end of this chapter, of a _solution_ to the problem of absurdity, not just the heroic acceptance of a problematic situation which we find in The Myth of Sisyphus, but an attempt to overcome that problem through an intense love of natural beauty.

Nonetheless, it remains true despite all this that the most lucid and explicit statement of absurdity in its grimmest outlines is contained in Camus' The Myth of Sisyphus, which we will consider the basic conception of absurdity.

The problem Camus addresses in The Myth of Sisyphus is quite simply whether there is any alternative to the absurdity of life besides suicide.

> There is but one truly serious philosophical
> problem, and that is suicide...The subject of
> this essay is precisely this relationship be-
> tween the absurd and suicide, the exact degree
> to which suicide is a solution to the absurd...
> Does the Absurd dictate death?[6]

For Camus absurdity is essentially the divorce of meaningful human thought from reality. The first awarenes absurdity, accordingly, is a sense of the strangeness and wonder of objects ordinarily wrapped in the familiarity of our own conceptual garb. Everything we had attributed to the world we now see as springing from ourselves. When we consider exactly what it is which we project on to the world, which in the experience of absurdity the world is perceived to be missing, we find in the absurdist literature two closely related answers, reason and meaning, and, corresponding to this, two related notions of absurdity--either a world without reason or things without meaningful identities. That is, what we supposed was part of the world but in the experience of absurdity suddenly discover to be part of ourselves, are the reasons we offer in explaining things in the world and the concepts by which we classify and thereby identify and recognize things in the world. Camus does not seem particularly concerned with this distinction, although it is very important to the later absurdists. But what he does say indicates pretty clearly that it is primarily the first of these two senses which he has in mind--absurdity as a world without reason.

Human beings are purposeful creatures, doing one thing for the sake of another and hence acting always, or usually, for a reason. So, we tend to transfer this way of thinking to the world itself, first interpreting objects in terms of their use to us and then, more generally, in looking for reasonable patterns of behavior on the part of the external world. But when we become more self-consciously critical, this process of "objectification" becomes strained, and we find it increasingly difficult to locate reason in the world. And then we suffer from the experience of absurdity.

The world we thereafter see for the first time as strange, new and alien or inhuman. Stripped of its idealized garb, the dense materiality of the world, the heavy side of absurdity, looms large.

A step lower and strangeness creeps in: perceiving that the world is "dense," sensing to what degree a stone is foreign and irreducible to us, with what intensity nature or a landscape can negate us. At the heart of all beauty lies something inhuman, and these hills, the softness of the sky, the outline of these trees at this very minute lose the illusory meaning with which we had clothed them, henceforth more remote than a lost paradise. The primitive hostility of the world rises up to face us across millennia. For a second we cease to understand it because for centuries we have understood in it solely the images and designs that we had attributed to it

beforehand, because henceforth we lack the power
to make use of that artifice. The world evades
us because it becomes itself again. That stage
scenery masked by habit becomes again what it is.
It withdraws at a distance from us.[7]

It is the successful projection of human thought upon t
world, naively seeing the world through a transparent c
ceptual frame we are not even aware of, which gives the
world its customary sense of familiarity. This "useful
artifice" is what Piaget calls "externalization." Like
Narcissus gazing into a pool, we see ourselves reflecte
in the world, and this gives the world a familiar, secu
and satisfying aspect. This is what we need and what w
normally get, and it is precisely this which the experi
of absurdity terminates.

> The mind's deepest desire...is an insistence upon
> familiarity, an appetite for clarity. Under-
> standing the world for a man is reducing it to the
> human, stamping it with his seal...The mind that
> arises to understand reality can consider itself
> satisfied only by reducing it to terms of thought.
> If man realized that the universe like him can
> love and suffer, he would be reconciled. If
> thought discovered in the shimmering mirrors of
> phenomena eternal relations capable of summing
> them up and summing themselves up in a single
> principle, then would be seen an intellectual joy
> of which the myth of the blessed would be a
> ridiculous imitation. That nostalgia for unity...
> But the fact of that nostalgia's existence does
> not imply that it is to be immediately satis-
> fied.[8]

The separation of thought from reality which the e
perience of absurdity brings about, therefore results i
sharp dualistic conception of the world, a split betwee
the human and the nonhuman, consciousness and physical
reality, essence and existence. Only within such a dua
ity could one analyse the experience of nostalgic longi
the failure of our desires to be fulfilled in reality,
things which ought to correspond, but don't.

> Of whom and of what indeed can I say: "I know
> that?" This heart within me I can feel; and I
> judge that it exists. This world I can touch, and
> I likewise judge that it exists. There ends all
> my knowledge, and the rest is construction.[9]

32

We know our own thoughts, and we cannot deny the existence of an external reality. That is, we have essence on one side and bare existence on the other. But how the two are related to one another we have no idea. And this is obviously a serious gap in our knowledge, for any knowledge of the world (as well as any meaningful experience of the world or any meaningful sense of being) requires seeing existing realities <u>as</u> or <u>in terms of</u> our conceptual essences. Absurdity, for Camus, is precisely the perception of this unbridgeable gap, that peculiar privative relation between the human desire to understand and the refusal of the world to accomodate us.

> What is absurd is the confrontation of this
> irrational [world] and the wild longing for
> clarity whose call echoes in the human heart.
> The absurd depends as much on man as on the
> world. For the moment it is all that links them
> together. It binds them one to the other as only
> hatred can weld two creatures together.[10]

The last part of this passage is interesting, for it suggests a bond, however tenuous, between the two terms of the absurdist duality. It is the tragic link, referred to earlier, and it is Camus' link with 19th century Romanticism. Absurdity is not a totally neutral vision of reality independent of all thought since it quite clearly implies a perception of the world as <u>lacking</u> what human thought demands. And, of course, to see the world in this problematic light is to see the world still through a human, indeed a Romantic point of view. Even as the gap between man and the world widens, the Romantic outlook tries more and more desperately, however hopeless the situation, to establish a sympathetic link with an increasingly alien and indifferent world. In this Romantic framework, I cry out to the world, but the world refuses to answer my cry and thus rejects and rebuffs me. It is like a lover's quarrel. But, however useless the attempt, I refuse to accept this rebuff and continue looking to the world for that sympathetic response I know I will never receive. Out of loyalty solely to myself and my humanistic ideals, I continue, like Sisyphus, a task which I know is doomed to failure. Later (chapter three) we will see how Robbe-Grillet tries to untie this last link to human subjectivity, removing the humanly tragic bias and exposing a totally neutral reality. "The world is neither meaningful nor meaningless," according to Robbe-Grillet; "it simply is."

It is this link which leads to Camus' conception of absurdity, which he defines as the relationship between man's desire for meaning and the world's lack of it.

It is a two-term relationship; absurdity is a property of
neither man nor the world alone, but of their confrontation

> I said before that the world is absurd, but I was
> too hasty. This world in itself is not reason-
> able, that is all that can be said. But what is
> absurd is the confrontation of this irrational
> [world] and the wild longing for clarity whose
> call echoes in the human heart.... Absurdity con-
> sists in the disproportion between intention and
> reality.... The magnitude of the absurdity will
> be in direct ratio to the two terms of my compar-
> ison.... Absurdity springs from a comparison.... The
> absurd is essentially a divorce. It lies in
> neither of the elements compared; it is born of
> their confrontation...The world is neither so
> rational nor so irrational. It is unreasonable
> and only that.... It is that divorce between the
> mind that desires and the world that disappoints....[11]

Interestingly, this account of absurdity is fully compatible with the meaning of the term in ordinary language,
whether French or English, as Camus demonstrates by several examples from everyday experience. In one such
example, Camus considers what we mean in ordinary speech
when we call absurd a lone man attacking a mob. It is,
just as in the philosophical analysis above,

> the disproportion between his intention and the
> reality he will encounter, of the contradiction I
> notice between his true strength and the aim he
> has in view. Likewise we shall deem a verdict
> absurd when we contrast it with the verdict
> the facts apparently dictate.[12]

Two important consequences follow from this definition of absurdity. First, as Camus asserts, it is not the
world itself which is absurd but only the world in relation to human expectations. Absurdity makes sense only in
terms of a human demand or expectation. As he says in a
passage quoted earlier, "the absurd depends as much on
man as on the world."

In these passages Camus indicates his awareness of an
important ambiguity which haunts most accounts of absurdity. Is absurdity the experience of reality stripped of
all humanly meaningful content, or the experience that
reality is independent of human thought? Absurdist writing, including Camus , frequently appears to assert the
former view of absurdity as a vision of "the naked World"

34

(Sartre). But this is clearly inconsistent. The whole
point about the experience of absurdity is that reality
transcends conceptual categories, that we can't perceive
reality as it is in itself. What absurdists mean, and
what they assert in more careful moments, is that we
become aware that thought and reality are distinct sorts
of things which don't automatically, necessarily or completely match up. The simplest, but also most misleading
way of expressing this is to talk of "the separation of
thought and reality," which taken in a too literal fashion
does suggest the experience of thought on one side and the
perception of a naked reality on the other. It is probably true that absurdists have themselves sometimes been
misled by their own form of words into thinking this was
what they meant. But in these passages at least, Camus
shows that he is aware of the ambiguity and sees which way
the account ought to go. On purely philosophical grounds
we would have to give Camus very high marks for this section of The Myth of Sisyphus.

To say that the world is absurd is not, therefore, the
same as saying simply that it is without reason or explanation. "Absurd" is an emotionally loaded word.
Robbe-Grillet is quite right about that. To call something
absurd is to criticise, condemn or denounce it, and this is
to suggest that it ought to be otherwise, that we justi-
fiably expect it not to be without reason or explanation.
So to say the world is absurd is not just to point out that
it is without reason or explanation, but also to perceive
that it lacks, or is missing reason and explanation. But
what exactly is the difference between something which
doesn't have a certain property and something which lacks
or is missing that property? This is in part what the
existentialist theory of negation is supposed to answer.

In the 1930's English-speaking philosophers had a
good laugh over Heidegger's assertion that "negation
negates not(hing)," as the prime example of philosophical
absurdity.[13] And out of context it is not perhaps as
clear as one would like. But the critics may have been
too hasty. The view which first Heidegger and then Sartre
tried to develop was that negation was not a fact about
the external world, but a peculiarly human way of perceiving things. Recall the picture-puzzles for children
in which one is asked to find what is missing in the picture. You are not asked simply to say what is not in the
picture--that would be too easy. If the picture shows
the interior of a house, you can truly say that there are
no mountains, elephants or locomotives in the picture. But
this is not what you are asked to find; you are asked to

35

discover what is missing and this means what ought to be
there but is not. You notice that a table has only three
legs and is therefore missing a fourth leg; you notice that
the door lacks a handle and so on. The point is that there
is no such thing as something's being missing aside from
the human conception (essence) of what ought to be there
or what we expect to find there. You glance at the table
and discover there are no dessert spoons, or in Sartre's
example considered in the first chapter, we look in at a
cafe and see that Peter's not there. The only person who
can meaningfully say, "Peter's not here tonight" is one who
knows that Peter usually frequents this cafe or promised to
be present on this particular night. It would be quite
pointless, for example, except as a bad joke, for me to
remark upon entering the cafe that Fidel Castro's not there.

So when Camus says the world is absurd, he means that
it lacks reason, that it is missing explanation. It is a
privative description, based on an unfavorable comparison
with the human world of reasons and explanations. In itself, Camus says, the world does not lack reason, that is,
it is not irrational; it simply doesn't have reason, that
is, it is simply not reasonable. This parallels the ordinary English distinction between what is amoral and what
is immoral (that is, immoral is to amoral what irrational
is to not reasonable). "Amoral" implies that it is not the
sort of thing which could be either moral or immoral;
whereas "immoral" implies that it is precisely the sort of
thing which assuredly ought to be, but alas is not, moral.
The idea of irrationality, then, is based on a privative
comparison with a world of human reason-giving; it suggests
that the external world ought to be reasonable, that we
somehow expect it to be reasonable.

This point is extremely important in discussing the
attempt to solve the problem of absurdity, particularly as
we find it in Beckett, by altering the human expectation.
As the ancient Stoics, whom Beckett frequently quotes,
argued, if a problem depends on human desire and that desire
is unreasonable, the problem can be removed by eradicating
the desire. The same strategy can also be found in Hindu
and Buddhist sources which absurdist writers occasionally
call upon for support. We can't change reality, but we can
change our relationship to that reality, especially, as
Beckett and occasionally Ionesco argue, if that expectation is not justified. So long as we demand that the world
be meaningful and it is not, we will be frustrated, clinging
to the Romantic, heroic posture of The Myth of Sisyphus and
"A Free Man's Worship." But why should the world be

36

reasonable? What right have we to expect this of an inanimate world, especially a world so completely nonhuman
as Camus and the other absurdists insist it is? Is that a
reasonable demand? Does it even make any sense? It may
turn out to be logically impossible for the thing-in-itself to have meaning!

Is it reasonable to suppose that the world is unreasonable and meaningless because it can only appear
meaningful to human beings? If we could imagine a world in
which there were no human beings (which Berkeley is right
in pointing out we cannot), there would not be the word,
concept or category of a tree and hence it would make no
sense to call that thing a tree. But that does not mean
that in the world as we actually find it that thing is not
a tree. Similarly, in the absence of people there would
be no such thing as Newton's Second Law of Dynamics, as
such, but that does not mean we can't explain things in
the world as we actually find it in terms of Newton's
Law. Because we assign meanings and give reasons, and do
this consistently and according to rules, the world is a
relatively reasonable and meaningful place. The world we
know is therefore a world of recognizable, meaningful
items bound together according to various reasons, interpretations, explanations. In themselves it may be true
that things are meaningless and reasons have no place, but
the world which we know and experience is by definition a
world which we interpret and understand in terms of human
concepts and essential forms of thought. The world in
itself is not something we could experience; the world
we can experience is by that very token a world we experience in terms of concepts and categories of thought.

Thus, to say that the world in itself is meaningless
and absurd is really a tautology; it is saying that the
world minus reason and interpretation is a world without
reason and interpretation. This, of course, is perfectly true, though we ought to add that it is unreasonable to expect or demand that the world in itself ought to
have reason and meaning. The world in itself can't have
reason and meaning, so it's unreasonable to suppose that it
ought to. In fact, when analyzed closely, it turns out
that the idea of a meaningful and reasonable world in
itself makes no sense whatever. On the other hand, to say
that the world we know and experience is reasonable and
meaningful is also a tautology; it is saying that the world
which we interpret and explain to ourselves is an interpreted and explainable world.

37

The second important consequence of Camus' definition
is that any attempt to drop one or other of the two terms
which define the problem is inadmissible as a solution to
the problem, and is indeed only an attempt to ignore or
cover it up. We must not deny the problem or pretend it
doesn't exist, Camus insists, but face it squarely, and
this means accepting both sides of the problem, human understanding and reality. Both parts of the problem must
be included in any assessment of absurdity because the
problem consists precisely in their relationship to one
another. Denying either distinctness from one another or
their relationship to one another is therefore to deny the
experience of absurdity. This forms the basis of Camus'
attack on both the existentialist solution of Kierkegaard,
Chestov and Jaspers and the phenomenological solution of
Husserl, the first for exaggerating the gap between man
and the world, the second for pretending it doesn't exist.
The existentialists deny the tragic relationship of thought
and reality; the phenomenologists deny the distinction
between thought and reality. Chestov, for example, argues
that because of the absolute gulf between man and the world
we are totally ignorant of the world, that the world is a
complete mystery, and thus effectively drops out of con-
sideration. At the opposite extreme, Camus argues, Husserl
simply defines the world as thoroughly and totally comprehensible to man. Thus, for Husserl as for Parmenides,
the world becomes synonymous with what is reasonable; while
for Kierkegaard, the world is so unreasonable, that we are
free to take that "leap of faith," embracing anything we
like, however irrational. The truth, Camus insists, lies
somewhere between these two extremes. Absurdity, as we
have seen, depends on the hope that the world is intelligible. But if that hope is to remain constant, it must be
a reasonable one, and to be a reasonable hope it must be
based on at least partial success in understanding the
world. Without the possibility of understanding the world
the absurd hope would simply be abandoned; without the
possibility of failure to understand the world the absurd
hope would never be thwarted as it is in the experience of
absurdity. Against Kierkegaard's "leap of faith," rejecting
reason and embracing irrationality, Camus argues,

> Our appetite for understanding, our nostalgia for
> the absolute are explicable only, in so far,
> precisely, as we can understand and explain many
> things. It is useless to negate the reason
> absolutely. It has its order in which it is
> efficacious.[14]

As we will see later, this is also an extremely telling

argument against Sartre's extremist position in Being and Nothingness.

Kierkegaard, therefore, "does not maintain the equilibrium" Camus insists upon as a necessary ingredient in absurdity between the desire to understand and the relative unintelligibility of the world. Kierkegaard, stressing man's frustrated longing to understand everything completely, embraces the subjective side of the problem, turning his back on the world we desire to understand. Husserl chooses the other side of the problem, construing the world as an extension of man's understanding intellect. Husserl thus makes his own leap of faith, determined to find intelligible essence in every object of consciousness--an act, for Camus, of "philosophical suicide."

> The absurd mind has less luck. For it the world
> is neither so rational [as Husserl claims] nor
> so irrational [as Kierkegaard maintains]. It is
> unreasonable and only that...In the universe of
> Husserl the world becomes clear and that longing
> for familiarity that man's heart harbors becomes
> useless. In Kierkegaard's apocalypse that desire
> for clarity must be given up if it wants to be
> satisfied.[15]

Thus both Kierkegaard and Husserl are guilty in opposite ways of a lack of balance, though Husserl appears to have realized this and in his last period tried desperately, though with questionable success, to redirect phenomenology away from its slide into idealism.[16] The absurd is a balance between two components: a desire for reason and the lack of reason in the world. Kierkegaard embraces the second as a positive statement of faith in the irrational; Husserl, at least in his most productive years, converts the first, the desire for reason, into a proof that the world is thoroughly reasonable. In neither case is there that tragic tension necessary to the experience of absurdity.

This is also the foundation of Camus' definition of tragedy, mentioned earlier, and his critique of Sartre for failing to maintain the proper tragic balance between man's hope and the world's reality. If our desire to understand the world were totally thwarted, there would be no problem how we could understand the world, nor, equally, if we always succeeded. The problem arises from the fact that we have an understanding of the world which we recognize is incomplete, or inaccurate. It is this realization which informs us that there is a difference between what we think the world is like and what the world really

is like. It would never occur to a solipsist that his vie
of things didn't correspond in some respects with reality.
Nor would this occur to an omniscient observer. Only when
knowledge breaks down, here and there, do we get the
distinction between the world and how we perceive the worl
We become aware of reality, not by seeing it as it is in
itself, but by becoming dissatisfied with our interpretations of reality.

This is the way the word "reality" functions in our
language, as well. Where there are conflicting accounts
of a given event, we ask, "What do you suppose really
happened? Will we ever know what was going on in reality?" This is the sort of question we all asked after
John Kennedy's assassination. What we meant is that altho
we knew what the reports stated, we weren't convinced
these reports "told it like it was," especially as different accounts varied considerably in their reconstructions
of that event. We assumed that something of a very definite and concrete nature did occur, and we wondered
whether these accounts of that event were accurate. What
we meant presupposes a contrast between what seemed to
happen and what really did happen. And that presupposes
at least this much metaphysics, that there are events in
the world and there are accounts or interpretations of
those events, and that these two can fall apart or at
least not "fit" very well.

Much of our ordinary talk about "real" and "reality"
presupposes, in other words, something like the Scholastic
distinction between thoughts about things and an independe
reality to which those thoughts may be directed. It also
implies the evaluative judgment that unless one intends to
tell a lie, day-dream, or talk about mythical entities, on
ought not to be satisfied with thoughts which only "loosel
fit reality, but must press toward a better fit.

Notice how important this use of "really" and "realit
is to us in expressing our ordinary views. There is something about us as people which these words articulate whic
makes possible a sense of dissatisfaction with the status
quo, the desire for a better world, speculation about the
future, and the gradual development and improvement in any
branch of knowledge. People, we may say, are like this.
They think they know certain things; they believe the worl
is like their description of it in certain respects. And
they have a certain confidence about this, But they are
also aware, here and there, that their account of the worl
is not perfect, that the world is not exactly as they say
it is, and occasionally, whether in lying or in simply bei

40

mistaken, not _at all_ as they say it is. And so they press
on trying to perfect their theories and interpretations.
This is the situation in which we all find ourselves, and
we express ourselves on this score by the use of locutions
like the ones above about what "really happened," or what
it's "really like."

It may be true, as followers of Husserl or Heidegger
would hold, that the world we know is a conceptual,
interpreted world, but it is also true that we can and
do have a sense of dissatisfaction with the falsity or
inaccuracy of some of our representations of the world,
and to that extent some sense of the real "thing itself" determines everyman's view of the world and his
relation to it. Consider the type of situation por-
trayed in the Japanese film _Rashomon_. The film concerns
a trial in a medieval Japanese court of law to determine
the circumstances in which a nobleman is killed by a
highwayman who then has sexual relations with the nobleman's bride. Was the man murdered or did he die in a
fairly fought duel? Was the wife forceably raped or
did she reject her husband and encourage the highwayman? Each witness to the event has a different version,
depending on his or her biased, self-interested standpoint, the highwayman claiming he killed the nobleman
in a duel after the woman encouraged his amorous
advances, and the ghost of the nobleman insisting that
he was treacherously murdered after being forced to
witness the rape of his wife by the highwayman. Yet
the judges rightly assume that only one concrete thing
happened, that the man was murdered or not, and that some
of the witnesses are more nearly accurate in their
statements than others. Indeed, without this assumption, the trial, like all trials, would be pointless.
This is not to say that the judges can find the truth;
sometimes they can't. But at least they _think_ they can,
and this belief determines their attitudes, behavior
and general stance vis-a-vis the objective world.

We can also become dissatisfied with the world as
we understand it, and any plan to improve upon it or any
fictional conception of a different and possibly better
world presupposes the contrast between thought and the
transcendent object of thought which terms like "reality"
help us to fix and preserve. We are capable of recogniz-
ing, in other words, both that our thoughts don't
(but ought to) fit reality and that reality doesn't
(but should) fit our hopes and desires. We see that the
world is neither just as we say it is nor precisely as
we think it should be, and so we are motivated by a

41

desire not only to improve upon our interpretations of the world, but, through change or in fiction, to improve upon the world as well.

This seems a reasonable account of certain ordinary ways of speaking and acting, and it also provides important insight into us as people, throwing off valuable hints and suggestions for philosophical anthropology. Generally, it seems part of the human situation always to have a limited, partial view of the world and to know it is limited and partial. If our interpretations of things are limited and partial, it follows first that the world as we know it is an interpreted world, a human achievement in some sense, and second that there is more to the world than our account of it--in short, a mutual independence of thought and reality.

Thus, Camus, like all absurdists, is a realist and a dualist, though not in a naive or simplistic way. Here, as elsewhere, Camus shows a more sophisticated awareness of the problem than he is generally credited. It might even be argued that in his rejection of the easy solutions of existentialism and idealistic phenomenology, Camus aligns himself with the most contemporary mood of philosophers of the 1970's returning to the tough, knotty problems of traditional philosophy. On the most literal level it appears that Camus and othe absurdists are arguing that there are two elements, thought and reality, essence and existence, totally distinct and bearing no relation to one another, like Parmenides' two "ways." And, in an effort to speak plainly and simply, this is the most plausible interpretation of many of their assertions taken at face value. It is also likely that the absurdists themselves are sometimes taken in by their own plain way of speaking. But here at any rate Camus makes it clear that he sees that this simplistic formula won't do, except heuristically as a very rough preliminary indicator. Without some link between thought and reality we would have no awareness of an external world, much less a worry over the extent of our understanding of it. To see that thought does not correspond with reality ironically but clearly presupposes that thought does correspond with reality at least some of the time. A mistaken perception, for example, can only occur in a context of presumably veridical perception. Only if the world appears as partially comprehensible can the doubt about its comprehensibility even arise. Nor, equally, if the world were completely comprehensible. In that case we would all be naive realists, simply identifying, or better, not distinguishing thought and reality; the world would just _be_ what it seems to us to be. Camus is therefore correct in his suggestion that the experience of absurdity must be within a prescribed balance between understanding the world and failing to understand it. By understanding reality partially and _knowing_ it is partial, we see the fundamental difference between an understanding _of_ reality and the reality of which it is an understand_ing_. But the fact that they are necessarily different sorts of things does not mean they are altogether unrelated. A picture of a dog is a very different sort of thing from a dog, but it is nonetheless _related_ to a dog by being a picture _of_ it. In a similar fashion Plato in _The Republic_ confuses the fact that a representation of a bed is not and cannot _be_ a bed with the quite different fact that it may or may not be a good _representation_ of a bed. As we will see later, Sartre fails to keep this distinction straight and so is led into confusions.

If we define absurdity as the disproportion between the world and our hopes and expectations, it is assumed that we are talking about reasonable hopes and expectations, hopes and expectations which could only be reasonable on the basis of some actual success, however partial. In the so-called "mystery" plays and novels of absurdist writers (e.g., Ionesco's _Victims of Duty_), this point is successfully exploited dramatically. Some question arises, and a solution is sought; there is no lack of clues, and evidence of all sort comes to the surface. Various plausible hypotheses emerge which clarify and explain--up to a point. But in the end each breaks down in some crucial flaw, and we are left without a single, comprehensible view of the total situation, as Mr. and Mrs. Martin discover in trying to determine whether they are man and wife in _The Bald Soprano_. It is not that the world is totally incomprehensible. On the contrary, the world is full of symbolic import; in fact, everything in the world points, suggests, implicates. It is just that it never adds up to a total picture. And it is this partially successful, partially unsuccessful attempt to understand the world which makes us aware that thought and object are different things which may or may not coincide.

It is also from the standpoint of balance that Camus criticises Sartre's idea of freedom, especially in _Nausea_ and the novels of the _Roads to Freedom_ trilogy. Man is free, according to Sartre, only in the sense that

he is totally and absolutely cut off from the world.
Men are unaffected by the world and in that sense are
free _from_ outside interference. But they are equally
not free to do anything in the world. Again, Camus is
surprisingly the more sophisticated of the two, and
closer to the truth. To be free requires being linked
to the world without being completely constrained by
the world, as R.M. Hare argues in his famous "paradox
of freedom."[17] As Camus points out, on Sartre's view
we are neither constrained nor linked, and this amounts
to a very odd sort of negative, useless freedom.

> [Sartre's] characters are, in fact, free.
> But their liberty is of no use to them...For
> in this universe man is free of the shakles of
> his prejudices, sometimes from his own nature,
> and, reduced to self-contemplation, becomes
> aware of his profound indifference to every-
> thing that is not himself. He is alone,
> enclosed in his liberty.[18]

Thus, Camus' notion of absurdity presupposes a
dualistic realism, though no absolute separation.
Thought and reality are distinct, though they can be mor
or less closely related. The two brought into prox-
imity makes for a meaningful, reasonable, familiar
world. The two relatively out of joint produces a
meaningless world experienced as absurd. It is precisely on this ground that Camus disagrees with Husserl.
For Husserl the world is the world constructed by human
thought. The world arises with and only with human
consciousness. This is the basis of Husserl's famous
refutation of Cartesian dualism, and with it the traditional mind-body problem and the supposed problem
of knowledge of the external world. As a human construction the world is thoroughly understandable; it
makes no sense, in this scheme, to speak of our understa
ing falling short of some transcendent reality. Therefore, there cannot be, in Husserl, any tragic reflection on the failure of thought to conform to reality.
That failure clearly depends, as Camus is aware, on a
duality of thought and a transcendent reality. At the
same time, however, Camus is not committed to the view
that we are somehow independently conscious both of our
own thoughts and of the "naked World" as distinct
objects of awareness. In fact he explicitly denies this
What he does say is that we become aware that there is a
distinction between the two, and this is obviously a
very different claim. It is one thing to see someone
naked and quite another to see that they are wearing

clothing. There is, for Camus, no transcendent reality of which we are completely ignorant; indeed what understanding we do possess is of various facets of reality. We understand reality, but not as it is in itself. Even where we do understand reality, reality and our understanding of it are not the same thing.

Interestingly, Camus' fiction is not as concerned with philosophical themes of absurdity as The Myth of Sisyphus and his other nonfiction works, the explanation for which probably has to do with the important distinction Camus draws in his article, "Herman Melville," between traditional novelists, like Melville (whom Camus particularly admires) in which ideas are expressed in images, and more recent novelists, such as Kafka, in which the images are the ideas.

> In Kafka, the reality that he describes is created by the symbol, the fact stems from the image, whereas in Melville the symbol emerges from reality, the image is born of what is seen.[19]

What I think Camus means by this is that in the traditional novel the image has been created by lifting real objects out of a context of ordinary perception and putting them to work in a new context in the work of fiction. Because of this, such images operate on at least two planes, the "manifest" plane of ordinary experience, and the "latent" plane of its new philosophical import in the novel. Thus, on one level, we have, in Moby Dick, an exciting fishing yarn, while on another level this becomes an image of man's search for the Absolute (or some such thing). In Kafka, on the other hand, the images only work on a philosophical level and thus become pure symbols. It is impossible, for example, to read Kafka's story of a man tickled to death by a newly developed writing machine as a documentary of political torture. Camus recognizes the limitations to metaphysical themes within the traditional style which he nonetheless prefers. Thus, on the whole, he consciously and wisely, perhaps, avoids metaphysical ideas in his fiction. Sartre, who also works mainly in the traditional manner, may be said for this reason to fail in many of his novels and plays precisely because of this limitation of the traditional novel. By the same token, Ionesco and Beckett have achieved far greater success in exploring metaphysical themes in fiction because they largely abandon the traditional form in favor of a writing style in which, as Camus says, the "reality is created by the symbol."

Where Camus does express philosophical ideas in fiction is probably best seen in The Stranger, in which Camus illuminates in terms of concrete human experience what it is like to face the world without any humanly projected illusions. Meursault appears incapable of ordinary human feeling; he is indifferent both to his mother's death and to the death of the Arab he has senselessly, almost accidentally killed. No one can understand Meursault's attitude, and as a result, everyone comes to despise him, not as a murderer, for whom in certain circumstances we might feel a degree of sympathy but for his cold and unfeeling lack of concern. But Meursault is unfeeling only in the sense that he refuses to conform to the social conventions of what is considered the appropriate feeling, i.e., that one should weep at one's mother's funeral and be contrite after an act of passion which results in another's death, even if that is not what one truly feels.

In this Meursault is an absurdist hero. The experience of absurdity is the experience of the separation of reality from all human projection. Ordinarily we blindly accept the conventional interpretation through which members of a particular society create and are thus able to share a commonly understood reality. To this socially constructed reality we have learned in turn how to respond in socially intelligible and acceptable ways. Achieving this comfortable and socially necessary conformity, of course, requires that each individual relinquish the peculiarities of his or her particular perspective. Most of us do this quite willingly, never realizing that these stereotyped responses are anything but expressions of our own unique and individual selves. Only the absurdist hero realizes this unconscious hypocrisy and, like Meursault, refuses to participate in the pretense.

The theme of the novel is not, then, as some critics have supposed, the dehumanizing effects of European nihilism, for which Meursault would have had the greatest contempt, but rather an odd sort of heroic posture in honestly and courageously facing the truth about a reality stripped of its familiar social guise. In order to locate this idea in images of everyday life Camus must find someone ordinarily capable of such extreme social indifference, and so he choses someone like Meursault as being more believable than, say, an intellectual of the kind Sartre selects for the central character in Nausea. Of the two Camus' is probably the

more successful as a work of literary fiction. In the
preface to the American University edition of L'Etranger
Camus himself wrote,

> The hero of my book is condemned because he
> does not stick to the rules. In this respect,
> he is foreign to the society in which he
> lives, he wanders, on the fringe, in the
> suburbs of private, solitary, sensual life.
> And this is why readers have been tempted to
> look upon him as a piece of social wreckage.
> A much more accurate idea of the character...
> will emerge if it is asked just how Meursault
> refuses to conform. The reply is a simple
> one: he refuses to lie. To lie is not only
> to say what is not the case. It also, above
> all, means saying more than is the case, and,
> as far as the human heart is concerned,
> more than we feel. It is what we all do,
> everyday to simplify life. He says what he is,
> he refuses to hide his feelings, and immed-
> iately society feels itself threatened...
> Meursault..., far from being empty of all
> feeling,...is inspired by a passion which is
> deep because it is stubborn, a passion for
> the absolute and for truth. This truth is
> still a negative one, the truth of what we
> are and what we feel, but without it no
> conquest of ourselves or of the world will
> ever be possible...L'Etranger [is] the story of
> a man who, with no heroics, accepts to die for
> truth.[20]

Or, as Meursault himself puts it at the end of the novel,

> Nothing, nothing had the least importance, and
> I knew quite well why... From the dark horizon
> of my future a sort of slow, persistent breeze
> had been blowing toward me, all my life long,
> from the years that were to come. And on its
> way that breeze had leveled out all the ideas
> that people tried to foist on me in the equally
> unreal years I then was living through... It
> was as if that great rush of anger had washed
> me clean, emptied me of hope, and gazing up at
> the dark sky spangled with its signs and stars,
> for the first time, the first, I laid my heart
> open to the benign indifference of the universe.
> To feel it so like myself, indeed, so brotherly,
> made me realize that I'd been happy, and that
> I was happy still.

47

The Stranger is not without its problems, however.
In order to make the central character believable, Camus
has selected a person whose indifference to social norms
is completely unlearned, unthinking, sensual and instinctual. In this way Camus avoids Sartre's problem in
Nausea of selecting an absurdist protagonist, Roquentin,
who is so intellectually conscious throughout the novel
of the metaphysical implications of his absurd situation
that the character is largely unbelievable--except as an
unemployed philosophy instructor. But by solving this
problem Camus finds himself faced with the opposite problem. If Meursault is totally unaware of the absurdist
grounds for his indifference, can he really be said to
be an absurdist? Is every antisocial person an absurdis
hero who "refuses to lie," who is "inspired by a passion
for the absolute and for truth," and who "accepts to die
for truth?" Clearly, the person who meets these descrip
tions is one whose indifference and stubborn antisocial
character spring from his realization of the gap between
his own individual perspective and the socially packaged
world offered up by his society--someone, in short, like
Sartre's Roquentin. But then would such a character be
believable as an ordinary human being, representative of
many of his type in society? Camus' solution to this
dilemma in The Stranger is to gradually increase
Meursault's awareness of the reasons for his stubborn
refusal to conform to socially approved norms so that
toward the end of the novel Meursault's reflection on
his plight, while in prison, eventually becomes a philosophical account of absurdity. But problems still haunt
either end of this psychological transition. In the
beginning of the novel is it believable that anyone but
a psychopath could be so genuinely and instinctively
indifferent to social pressures without an alternative
intellectual rationale? And is it believable toward the
end of the novel that such an instinctual man could so
quickly become a philosopher? Perhaps, as we shall see
later on, these problems simply cannot be completely
overcome within the framework of the traditional realist
novel, the novel form in which, as Camus says, philosophical ideas are expressed in images.

      In summary, Camus provides us with a remarkably
clear and reasonably accurate definition of absurdity as
the perception of the divorce of thought from reality, t
clashing dissonant relation between these two terms. Th
offers a convenient point of departure for our discussio
of further developments of this fundamental concept by
other absurdist writers which we shall consider in
subsequent chapters. One such development is the

characterization of the object stripped of human meaning. Camus has little to say about this, far less than Sartre, Ionesco and Beckett, though on the whole he seems to perceive a world without meaning as a heavy, dense materialism. Nor does Camus appear nearly as concerned as other absurdists with the problem of language detached from the world. Indeed Camus' position is Romantic in many ways. We reach out to communicate with the world and are tragically rebuffed, but even this rebuff is a kind of communication. Language, for Camus, is never completely detached from the world, floating free, "on holiday," as Wittgenstein once said.

It is also in Romantic terms that Camus occasionally speaks of a kind of solution to absurdity which we should mention in closing. At times Camus refers to an experience of natural beauty which overcomes the tragic frustration of trying to remake the world in our own image. In this Romantic and aesthetic, and almost mystical vision, the world is accepted on its own terms, neither meeting nor denying our demands upon it, but transcending those demands altogether. Since those demands are not frustrated, the tragic problem of absurdity is overcome, though apparently only in rare moments for Camus. Later we will see this solution developed, first in Ionesco and then more thoroughly in Beckett, as a positive, hopeful and constructive side to absurdity.

At first Camus finds only a wary truce between man and nature as between two watchful enemies.

> Everyday he went off into the mountains and came back speechless...When he reached the distant summit and saw the immense countryside stretching out before him, he felt not the calm peace of love but a kind of inner peace which he was signing with this alien nature, a truce concluded between two hard and savage faces, the intimacy of enemies rather than the ease of friendship.[21]

But there is also an experience Camus mentions in the Notebooks in which the self-important humanistic and romantic demands made upon the world are transcended and the sheer beauty and wonder of the world absorbs all consciousness, replacing everything--including the humanistically inflated importance of ourselves, standing arrogant, hurt, and defiant against the world.

We lead a difficult life, not always managing
to fit our actions to the vision we have of
the world....But a day comes when the earth
has its simple and primitive smile. Then,
it is as if the struggles and life within us
were rubbed out. Millions of eyes have looked
at this landscape, and for me it is like the
first smile of the world. It takes me out of
myself....It denies me a personality, and
deprives my suffering of its echo. The world
is beautiful and this is everything. The
great truth which it patiently teaches me is
that neither the mind nor even the heart has
any importance....The world reduces one to
nothing....Without anger, it denies that I
exist. And, agreeing to my defeat, I move
toward a wisdom...except that tears come into
my eyes, and this great sob of poetry which
swells my heart makes me forget the truth of
the world.[22]

NOTES

1. Albert Camus. "Three Interviews," in Lyrical
and Critical Essays, Philip Thody, ed., Ellen Conroy
Kennedy, trans. (New York: Alfred A. Knopf, 1969),
p. 346.

2. Camus, Notebooks 1935-1942, Philip Thody, trans.
(New York: Alfred A. Knopf, 1969), p. 25.

3. Camus, "On the Future of Tragedy," in Lyrical
and Critical Essays, op. cit., p. 304.

4. Camus, "On Jean-Paul Sartre's La Nausee," Ibid.,
p. 201.

5. Ibid.

6. Camus, The Myth of Sisyphus, Justin O'Brien, tra
(New York: Vintage Books, 1955), pp. 3-7.

7. Ibid., p. 11.

8. Ibid., p. 13.

9. Ibid., p. 14.

10. Ibid., p. 16.

11. Ibid., pp. 16-37.

12. Ibid., p. 21.

13. Rudolf Carnap, "The Elimination of Metaphysics Through Logical Analysis," Arthur Pap, trans., in Logical Positivism, A. J. Ayer, ed. (New York: The Free Press, 1959), p. 69.

14. Camus, The Myth of Sisyphus, op. cit., p. 28.

15. Ibid., p. 36.

16. Major criticisms of Husserlian idealism include Rudolf Boehm, "Husserl und der Klassische Idealismus," in Vom Gesichtspunkt der Phänomenologie, (Martinus Nijhoff, 1968); Joseph Kockelmans, Edmund Husserl's Phenomenological Psychology (Duquensne University Press, 1967); Ludwig Landgrebe, Major Problems in Contemporary European Philosophy (Ungar, 1966); Maurice Merleau-Ponty, Phenomenology of Perception (Humanities Press, 1962); Anna-Teresa Tymieniecka, Why is There Something Rather the Nothing (Van Gorcum, 1966); Theodor Celms, Der Phänomenologische Idealism Husserls (Riga, 1928); Roman Ingarden, Der Streit um die Existenz der Welt (Max Niemeyer Verlag, 1964-1966; Paul Ricoeur, Husserl, An Analysis of his Phenomenology (Northwestern University Press, 1967).

17. R. M. Hare, Freedom and Reason (Oxford: Oxford University Press, 1963), p. 1.

18. Camus, "On Sartre's Le Mur and Other Stories," Lyrical and Critical Essays, op. cit., p. 205.

19. Camus, "Herman Melville," Ibid., p. 293.

20. Ibid., pp. 251-252.

21. Camus, Notebooks 1935-1942, op. cit., p. 45.

22. Ibid., p. 56.

CHAPTER THREE: SARTRE

Sartre is by far the most philosophical of the
writers we will consider. Besides being a novelist, a
playwright, a critic and a social commentator, Sartre
is also a professional philosopher. There is in Sartre's
writings, therefore, the clearest link between philosophical ideas and fictional images--in Camus' opinion,
as we have seen, far too great a link. That is, in
Sartre there is a deliberate and direct translation of
philosophical ideas into fiction. In other absurdists
one finds suggestions of philosophical import in the
fiction and then discovers some corroboration here and
there in nonfiction works which are partially but not
exclusively philosophical in nature. With Sartre, on
the other hand, one can locate the same idea developed
fictionally, say in Nausea or No Exit, as had previously
been articulated philosophically, say in Being and
Nothingness. What is doubtful about Sartre's literary
works, as Camus points out, is that the ideas have not
been worked out fictionally, but are simply philosophical ideas dressed up as fiction. On the assumption
that fictional content must be transformed by fictional
form and not simply translated into it (see chapter
one), Sartre's literary output is not as artistically
compelling as that of Camus, Ionesco or Beckett. Indeed,
as we will see, it is only with radical changes in the
form of the novel and play that the metaphysical content
of Ionesco's and Beckett's work becomes so persuasive
and exciting as art.

Nonetheless, from a philosophical point of view, the
comparison of Sartre's philosophical writing with his
fiction proves both interesting and illuminating. Our
plan in this chapter, then, will be to look first at
Being and Nothingness and then at Nausea, the most philosophical of his fiction works, to see how absurdity is
first defined and then concretely located within human
experience.

Prior to Being and Nothingness, Heidegger introduced two new notions of nothingness into an already
bewildering maze of traditional conceptions, and these
new notions are important in understanding Sartre. In
the first sense nothingness is the gap between man and
the world (consciousness and what we are conscious of)
which, in our discussion, is simply another name for
absurdity in its simplest form. In Heidegger's second

sense, nothingness is the evaporation of objects from th
world, which we understand in the context of our discussion as the light aspect of the response to absurdity.
The first is an epistemological awareness of, the second
an emotional response to the distinction between thought
and object, essence and existence.[1] Being and Nothingness is an exploration of the first; Nausea a fictional
account of the second.

But this notion of a gap between man and the world
presupposes a metaphysical and epistemological dualism
in Sartre which is highly problematic. Philosophically,
Sartre is, or was when he wrote Being and Nothingness,
a phenomenologist, and the hallmark of phenomenology
is its repudiation of dualism, especially the mind-
body dualism of Descartes. This, along with the attend-
ant problems of freedom and determinism, and knowledge
of the external world, pretty well define the scope of
modern philosophy. A widespread conception of the task
of philosophy at the turn of the century in Britain,
America and on the Continent was the rejection of dualis
Prominent examples include Dewey's concept of "experience" as an inseparable synthesis of thought and the
object of thought, and Moore's famous "refutation of
idealism" based on a similar synthesis, though independently derived. But above all, this defines the task
of phenomenology in its early years. How then can Sartr
be both a phenomenologist and a dualist?

Like Dewey and Moore earlier, phenomenologists
distinguish thought and object simply as two poles or
sides of a single organic unity, the intentional act.
Since each requires the other, and neither can exist
apart from the other, there is a distinction but no
dichotomy between thought and its object. In Hume's
language, they are distinguishable but not separable.
This might be symbolized (T-O). Sartre accepts this
notion and makes use of it in his own refutation of
Cartesian dualism: thought can't be removed from its
object in any fundamental way since without its object
there is no thought. Where there is thought there is an
object of thought; if you think you must think something
an argument Plato had used much earlier to prove the
existence of Ideas (to think about ideal justice, there
must be an ideal justice, even though it can't exist
in the spatio-temporal physical world).

But Sartre also wants a notion of the object as
being more independent of thought (that is, "real," in

the traditional sense), and this leads to a sharper
split between thought and object. A real object, of
course, can exist independently of any thought, and in
the case of mistakes, fantasies and the like, thought
can go its own way independently of reality. The object
in this sense we will call the real object and symbolize
its relation to the other object (the intentional
object): (T-O) - R. In terms of our earlier discussion,
the intentional object designates being as essence, while
the real object corresponds to being as existence. It
is around this ambiguity between the intentional object
and the real object that difficulties arise in trying to
understand Sartre.   To think is to think about something. So you can't think without a something to think
about. But is this "something" the object as it appears
to you or the object as it is independently of your, or
anyone else's, thought of it? Sartre wants both, and
he distinguishes the two in Being and Nothingness as the
"phenomenon of being" (the intentional object) and the
"being of phenomena" (the real object).

     In this sense, then, Sartre is a realist and a dual-
ist.   To a certain extent this is, like Camus, a deliberate rejection of the tendency in Husserl and Heidegger
toward idealism, but it is also, at least partly, a
dualism despite himself. Sartre would really like to
have it both ways--avoiding both idealism and dualism.
Indeed the major stated purpose of Being and Nothingness is to differentiate nonhuman being (being-in-itself)
from human being (being-for-itself) without falling
into Cartesian dualism. But, somewhat like Locke toward
the end of the Essay, Sartre has considerable difficulty demonstrating at the end of Being and Nothingness
that the two regions of being are held together in any
sort of meaningful synthesis. Since the two are said
to be synthesized only in the weak sense that both can
be included in a third, very broad category, Sartre
cannot be said to have succeeded. Dualistic pairs
always belong to some common category, if only in the
sense that this is what they are dualistic pairs of.
As Ryle points out in Concept of Mind, Cartesian dualism
requires placing both Mind and Body in the same category
of substance (a category mistake, on Ryle's view).
Since this sort of synthesis is required by dualism,
it is not a sufficient shield against the charge of
dualism. Descartes himself could claim this sort of
synthesis of mind and body; since both are substances,
he might argue, substance joins them together in a new
unity. The two terms of any duality exist necessarily
but trivially within the larger vacuuous sphere of

55

whatever it is which their dichotomy has split in two. In Sartre's case it is the most vacuuous of all categories, "pan", all there is. What is required for a genuine synthesis which would avoid dualism is a sense in which the two functionally require or interact with each other, as in the thought-object synthesis of intentionality. Thought needs an object because the very nature of thought is to be the thought of an object; and an object of thought needs thought because in order to be an object of thought it must, by definition, be capable of being thought. Indeed, as we have seen all along, this is the sort of synthesis required to have a meaningful world, and a full sense of being, along the lines derived from Aristotle, a genuine link between our conceptions and reality, that is, between essence and existence. But this synthesis is nowhere to be found in Sartre, nor can we imagine how he could overcome the radical dualism of Being-in-itself and Being-for-itself.

There is no great mystery about a dualist trying to avoid dualism. It happens frequently. Spinoza solved Cartesian dualism by treating Descartes' two created substances, mind and matter, simply as attributes of a single substance. But then a new dualism sprang up within his philosophy, between the one substance and its many modes. Dualisms are very hard to get rid of; certainly they don't disappear simply by fiat. Many philosophers today are reluctantly coming to the conclusion that the grandiose plans of the 1950's for ending all dualisms once and for all must now be abandoned as overly simplistic. Thus, despite Sartre's attempt, the old dualism of Descartes, Locke and Kant between thought and reality, essence and existence simply reemerges in Being and Nothingness as the duality of Being-in-itself and Being-for-itself.

The phenomenologists have not then avoided the ancient dilemma we noted earlier in discussing Aristotle between idealism and realism, or, since realism implies dualism, the dilemma between idealism and dualism. Thus far the synthesis of essence and existence has only been achieved within an idealist standpoint. In rejecting dualism Husserl and Heidegger gravitate toward idealism, while Sartre, in rejecting idealism, inevitably moves toward dualism. Because of the inseparability of thought and object in the intentional act, the object of thought becomes necessarily intelligible, through and through. Thus Camus' criticism we saw

earlier that it is too "rational". For Husserl everything can be separately bracketed and made an object of
investigation. Thus, anything, including reality, being,
and the world, can become a meaningful object of thought.
For Sartre, on the contrary, the being of phenomena,
the ultimate ground of what appears to us in consciousness, cannot be bracketed and therefore transcends
understanding, somewhat like Aristotle's prime matter.

Heidegger's theory of being follows Husserl in
rejecting the traditional contrast between real and ideal
being, reality and appearance. Heidegger's notion of
being concerns the contrast between meaning, which includes both real and apparent being, on one side, and
nothingness on the other side. Being is whatever can
be comprehended as something, that is, interpreted in
terms of some conceptual framework. Even fictional
entities, dreams and mirages are understood as something.
They have identifiable essence, if not real existence.
Being, for Heidegger, in other words, is essence or
being-as. Nothingness, for Heidegger, is not, therefore,
nonexistence, but nonessence, that is, the meaninglessness of things.

Like Sartre, John Wild disagrees with Heidegger that
being is coextensive with meaning. While Wild admits
that the world we are aware of is a humanly interpreted
world, coextensive with meaning, he argues that this is
only possible against the broader back drop of a "world-
horizon" which includes both understood reality and
reality which awaits, or needs to be understood.

> Being is not necessarily joined with meaning as
> the major stream of Western thought, and also
> Heidegger, have supposed. Contrary to these
> teachings they may fall apart, and they may have
> fallen apart in the world of our time.[2]

It seems to me the realists, Sartre, Wild and Camus, are
right. We need a concept of a reality which is not
understood to explain the world we do understand.
Husserl and Heidegger are right to insist on the priority
of intelligible being, the priority, that is, of being
as the synthesis of thought and reality. But they are
wrong in ignoring the important question of the relation
of the understood world to an independent reality. As
the Zen Buddhists say, we must not mistake the finger
which points for the moon to which it points. Meaning
and being, essence and existence, are not identical.
Thus, unfortunately, all the problems of dualism remain;

how can we determine whether our interpretations of the world really "tell it like it is?"

At the outset of Being and Nothingness Sartre states his aim as overcoming the appearance-reality dualism by "the monism of the phenomenon."[3] Nonetheless, as he admits, his account eventually reverts to "a new dualism: that of finite and infinite,"[4] by which he means something like appearance and reality, things as we understand them and things as they are in themselves. As John Stuart Mill said, an object appears in perception in only one finite way at a time, though we are aware that there are infinitely many more ways in which the object could appear. There is, therefore, an ambiguity in Sartre's notion of being which he tries to clear up at the beginning. Being refers either to understood being ("phenomenon of being") or to a transcendent reality which always stands outside thought ("being of phenomena"). The phenomenon of being is being as it appears, that is, describable being, being under some human interpretation, while the being of phenomena is indescribable, it just is. In the latter sense,

> Being is neither one of the object's qualities, capable of being apprehended among others, nor a meaning of the object....The object does not possess being, and its existence is not a participation in being....It is. That is the only way to define its manner....It is being-for-revealing and not revealed being....Knowledge cannot by itself give an account of being; that is, the being of phenomena cannot be reduced to the phenomenon of being.[5]

In terms of our discussion, the phenomenon of being is essence and the being of phenomena is existence. Insofar as we can talk about it, locate it among other concepts and even define it, being has a comprehensible essence (like substance in Aristotle). But insofar as being transcends the thinking subject, it cannot enter thought in any way (like Aristotle's notion of prime matter).

The problem, like that of Plato and Aristotle before him, is in reconciling these opposed conceptions. As Klaus Hartmann puts it in his penetrating book, Sartre's Ontology,

58

The resulting division of beings (existents)
is into subjective being and the being of
phenomena. Sartre's ontology is based on
this division...It must contain an elucidation
of the relation between members of this dis-
junction.[6]

But this is going to be very difficult to accomplish. Ironically, by identifying the understood object
as the intentional object, Sartre opens an even wider
gap between the real object and thought. Through his
distinction of the intentional object and the real
object, Sartre has made it a matter of necessity that
the intentional object be thoroughly understood while
the real object remain completely beyond understanding,
thus widening the gap between thought and reality and
making any reconciliation well nigh impossible. As
Sartre tries to show in Nausea, because of the mutual
split between thought and the real object, the object
could literally be anything, while we, on the other side
of the dichotomy, can also be anything and are hence
absolutely free. In other words, the two are so far
apart, neither exerts the slightest influence or limitation on the other. This is reminiscent of Stoic
freedom, based on a similarly extreme Socratic duality
of mind and body. We can say what we like of reality,
but reality pays not the slightest heed. And whatever
the world is like, we are free from any interference
from it. In Husserlian language, Sartre resists the
idea that the world itself can be bracketed. As Mary
Warnock says,

He objects...to the whole idea of the phenomenological "epoche," the putting of the world
inside brackets....For, he argues, things in
the world just will not submit to being bracketed. They exist, fully, and as obstacles to
ourselves...It may well seem that Sartre's
objection to Husserl is rather like Dr.
Johnson's refutation of Berkeley's idealism,
the refutation by kicking a stone.[7]

Thus the realist split in Sartre's ontology between
thought and reality, essence and existence, or as he calls
it in Being and Nothingness, "Being-for-itself" and
"Being-in-itself." The entirety of Sartre's elaborate
analysis of this distinction turns on the relatively
simple relation of "transcendence." "Consciousness is
consciousness of something. This means that transcendence

59

is the constitutive structure of consciousness."[8]   If
thought is <u>of</u> an object, then it transcends that object.
That is, there are things in the world and there are conceptions and interpretations <u>of</u> things.   This doesn't
mean that thoughts are not things too, but that they
always operate on a second level directed at other
things on the first level.   Similarly with representational pictures or stories, insofar as the stories
are <u>about</u>, or <u>of</u> something besides themselves, they
have a self-transcending nature.   All the rest of the
contrast between being-in-itself and being-for-itself
is implied in this transcendence.

     Thought is always directed or related, for example,
to something beyond itself; reality is not.   It also
follows from the notion of transcendence that thought
exists <u>only</u> <u>in</u> this relation to the object; it has no
self-existence, which the real object does.   Similarly,
thought has no nature or content of its own.   Again,
it is strictly parasitic on the object.   As Sartre
insists, thought is not the presence of the object to
an already existing thought, but the reverse, the presence of thought to an object of thought.   This is just
the reverse of the idealist worry over the impermanence
of the object, that is, whether it exists if we are
not thinking of it.   For Sartre, the problem is whether
there is anything to thought apart from its transcendence
to the object.   This resembles Hume's analysis of consciousness.   Do we have an idea of what thinking is
like, Hume asks?   No; whenever we introspect upon our
thinking we find only various objects of thought.
Similarly, Moore in his refutation of idealism argues th
consciousness is nothing but the form of our thought;
the content is always the object of thought.   Of
course, thought could itself become an object of though
which Sartre sometimes seems to ignore.   But even so,
<u>as</u> <u>such</u>, it is no longer thought but the object of
thought.   The active thinking cannot be the object of
its own act of thought.   Finally it follows from the
idea of transcendence that in thinking <u>of</u> an object we
must think of it in terms of what it is not.   That is,
think of X is to think of X as A, and <u>not</u> B, C or D.

     Thought attributes categories to the object, and
hence conceives it in terms of its comparison with other
objects; it is like some but not like others.   Hence
attribution to an object always implies negation. To
say X is a tree is to say it is not a stone, or a chimp-
anzee, and so on.   Also, since there is always more to
the object than can appear to consciousness at any one

60

instant, what the object is at any given moment is related by thought to what it can become but is not at the moment. The tree is perceived in terms of its possibilities for firewood, potential farm plot, and so on. Essential to thought, therefore, is its relating the object to what it is not (other objects and future possibilities), a theory very similar to empiricist accounts, like that of C. I. Lewis, for relating the sensation of a momentary appearance to the perception of an object. None of this holds true of the real object, which has no interest in its relation to anything. Indeed, in itself it has no relations to anything beyond itself. We relate things according to our interests; there are no relations in reality.

Hence, being-in-itself, having no intrinsic connections with anything else, is essentially without meaning or reason. It just is; wholly gratuitous, and, in an odd way, atomistic in its absolute isolation from everything else. Hence we can never know the real object; to know X is to convert it into an essence, looking at only one aspect among many, and relating what is essentially nonrelational. This is an ancient legacy, as we have seen, but more immediately it is the legacy of the Kantian epistemology, that we can only understand reality by humanizing and thereby distorting it.

All Sartre's descriptions of the distinction between being-in-itself and being-for-itself revolve around these characteristics, though, for reasons we will examine shortly, Sartre focuses on the negative character of thought--hence the title of the book, Being (being-in-itself) and Nothingness (being-for-itself). Being-in-itself, Sartre argues, is transphenomenal, that is, it is independent of thought.

> It is the being of this table...It requires
> simply that the being of that which appears
> does not exist only insofar as it appears.
> The transphenomenal being of what exists for
> consciousness is itself in itself....The pri-
> mary characteristic of the being of an exist-
> ent is never to reveal itself completely to
> consciousness....Consciousness can always pass
> beyond the existent, not toward its being, but
> toward the meaning of this being....(Thus we)
> distinguish two absolutely separated regions
> of being....Being is in itself....Being is at
> bottom beyond the self....Being is opaque to
> itself precisely because it is filled with

itself...the being of for-itself is defined,
on the contrary, as being what it is not and
not being what it is....Being is isolated in
its being and...does not enter into any connection with what is not itself....It is, this
is what consciousness expresses in anthropomorphic terms by saying that being is superfluous (de trop)...uncreated, without reason
for being, without any connection with another
being.[9]

Real being, then, is meaningless. Meaning comes
only with human attribution, and this is possible only
with the assignment of one thing to another, hence
relations; and relations are only possible with negation. Hence for Sartre, negation is the essential char
acter of human consciousness. Much of Sartre's way of
putting this is inexcusable mystificaiton; but much of
it can be translated into a sensible, important and
largely correct analysis of human thought. A clearer,
though possibly less exciting, account of this aspect
of consciousness has already been given by the American
pragmatists, with whom both Sartre and his mentor,
Heidegger, show great affinity. Whatever the source,
let's look at this sensible "grain of truth" in Sartre'
difficult claims about man's nothingness.

Human thought is seldom, if ever, a blank staring,
as Descartes seems to have thought. We are purposeful
creatures, doing one thing for the sake of another.
And this capacity translates into human perception and
thought. We tend to see an object in terms of its
function or use, in terms of what it can and cannot do
for us. Every momentary perception of an object, there
fore, is filled out by expectations in terms of what is
not present, but which could become so if we act or
fail to act in certain ways. Crossing a street I
catch a glimpse of a car coming toward me. It is not
idle curiosity that I see it as a car. I see the car
now in terms of what will happen to me in the immediate
future if I do not take care to get out its way. Once
out of the way, I catch sight of a bus, a bus which is
potential means of getting me to my destination if I
take the appropriate action to get on it. Upon reflection, we can see that the "infinitude" of an object, as
opposed to the "finitude" of its present appearance,
consists largely if not entirely of these purposive
or anthropomorphic possibilities. But oddly perhaps,
this means that we see things mostly in terms of what
they are not. As Hume said, an object is composed main

of imagination. As a thought experiment, consider how much
of your thought each day is concerned with things which do
not exist (past, future, hopes, plans, dreams, etc.). X is
of interest to me mainly in terms of what it may bring in
the future. But by definition the future does not exist,
so my interest in the object is in terms of what it is not,
but might become if I take the appropriate action. It is
only through this aspect of human thought that "nothing"
and "not" enter the world. As we saw in our cafe example
in the last chapter, there is no nothing in reality, there is
nothing only relative to human expectation. Likewise, of
course, there is no essential something without some limitation, or "determination," as Hegel calls it, and this too
implies the concept of "nothing." To be A is not to be B, C,
or D. As Sartre says,

> Non-being always appears within the limits of a
> human expectation. . . The world does not dis-
> close its non-being to one who has not first
> posited them as possibilities.[10]

> There is not the slightest emptiness in being,
> not the tiniest crack through which nothingness
> might slip in. The distinguishing characteristic
> of consciousness, on the other hand, is that it
> is a decompression of being. Indeed, it is
> impossible to define it as coincidence with
> itself.[11]

As Sartre acknowledges, Heidegger had already analyzed
consciousness along these lines, though positively, in terms
of man's "being-in-the-world" through throwness, concern and
projection, using objects as tools (das Zeug) "for the sake
of" our projects and concerns. For Heidegger man is
essentially a being whose existence is to understand and
interpret himslef and his world. "Dasein is an entity
which, in its very Being, comports itself understandingly
toward that Being."[12] This basic feature of man Heidegger
calls his "being-in the-world." Man is the kind of thing
which must live in a familiar, interpreted world. Being-
in-the-world, then, is composed of various human concerns,
and this presupposes our ability to relate to objects in
terms of our interests and needs, being able to see them as
objects which can meet or thward those needs. This is our
primary cognitive relation to things in the world, according
to Heidegger; not a theoretical curiosity, but a practical
concern with objects which "manipulates things and puts
them to use."[13] Thus in our everyday attitude we see things
as tools, instruments "for writing, sewing, working, trans-
portation, measurement;" things are "essentially 'something
in-order-to'. . . ."[14] Thus we project from our human stand-

point a purposive relation on things, fixing them as mea
to some human end, an "assignment or reference of someth
to something."[15] We understand a pencil, for example, h
relating it to the purpose or end of writing; this is ho
it takes its place in the phenomenal world of our concer

> As understanding, <u>Dasein</u> projects its Being
> upon possibilities . . . The projecting of
> the understanding has its own possiblity--
> that of developing itself [which] we call
> "interpretation," . . . the working out of
> possibilities projected in understanding . . .
> We "see" it <u>as</u> a table, a door, a carriage,
> or a bridge . . . In the mere encountering
> of something, it is understood in terms of
> a totality of involvements and . . .
> assignment-relations. . . In the projecting
> of the understanding, entities are disclosed
> in their possibility . . .[16]

Sartre, however, prefers to describe this process b
its negative, rather than its positive, designation.

> The characteristic of Heidegger's philosophy
> is to describe Dasein by using positive terms
> which hide the implicit negations. Dasein is
> "outside of itself, in the world," . . . it
> is "its own possibilities," etc. All this
> amounts to saying that Dasein "is not" in
> itself . . .[17]

Why does Sartre prefer this negative characterization?
Sartre is quite right that negation is only possible wi
human thought. "What must man be in his being in order
that through him nothingness may come into being?"[18] A
a transcendental analysis of the possibility of negatio
Sartre's account is basically correct. He is also corr
in his analysis of thought in terms of possibilities, w
in turn imply negation. And there are other interestin
ways in which negation enters the picture which we ough
to consider briefly.

> In the transcendence of consciousness thought is r
vealed as <u>not</u> being reality and reality is revealed as
<u>not</u> being thought.

> If man adopts any particular behavior in the face
> of being-in-itself . . . it is because he is <u>not</u>
> this being. We discover non-being as a condition
> of the transcendence toward being.[19]

> What is present to me is what is not me...
> The thing, before all comparison, before
> all construction, is that which is present
> to consciousness as <u>not</u> <u>being</u> consciousness.[20]

> Being is revealed as not being the for-itself...
> It appears <u>outside</u> <u>the</u> <u>for-itself</u>, beyond all
> reach, as that which determines the for-itself
> in its being.[21]

Also, because thought is mere transcendence, it adds <u>nothing</u>
to being. "It does not enrich being, for knowledge is pure
negativity. It only brings it about that <u>there</u> <u>is</u> being.
But this fact . . . is not an inner determination of being --
which is what it is -- but of negativity."[22] Elsewhere
Sartre describes thought as a decompression of being. There
is also <u>nothing</u> <u>to</u> thought but its aboutness in relation
to the object. When we are conscious of something we
may or may not be conscious of being conscious of it. Even
where we are, there is no content to this consciousness
<u>of</u> consciousness but its character of "aboutness" or
transcendence. Where we are conscious of something without
being conscious <u>of</u> that consciousness, our consciousness
is totally absorbed in its object, losing itself therein
in a way Heidegger calls our "fallenness" in the object,
reducing itself to <u>nothing</u>.

> A psychological and empirical exemplification
> ...is...the case of <u>fascination</u>. In fascina-
> tion...the knower is absolutely nothing but
> a pure negation; he does not find or recover
> himself anywhere--he is <u>not</u>. The only qual-
> ification which he can support is that he is
> <u>not</u> precisely this particular fascinating
> object....I am precisely the immediate
> negation of the object and nothing but that.[23]

And finally, as we saw in Aristotle, we can understand an object only by reducing it from a real being
to an understood being. That is, only by reducing
existence to essence. Thus thought loses itself in
the object, and the object loses its reality in
thought.

> But while being in-itself is contingent, it re-
> covers itself by degenerating into a for-
> itself. It <u>is</u>, in order to lose itself in a
> for-itself. In a word, being <u>is</u> and can only
> be.[24]

That which is annihilated in consciousness...
is the contingent in-itself....As soon as I
consider this totality in in-itself, it nihilates
itself under my regard....This perpetually
evanescent contingency of the in-itself which,
without ever allowing itself to be apprehended,
haunts the for-itself and reattaches it to
being-in-itself--this contingency is what
we shall call the facticity of the for-
itself.[25]

We can't grasp being-in-itself, yet it "haunts"
us, taunts us like the carrot just out of reach by the
donkey in one of Sartre's more colorful illustrations.[26]
Facticity is the link with the experience of nausea, to
which we will return shortly. It is the contingency
of the thing-in-itself which suggests to us that we
too are materially contingent and can become nothing.
We can't grasp the thing-in-itself, but by way of contrast with understood being, we have some regulative
concept, or "limiting concept," as Sartre describes
it, of pure facticity--that reality is not this or that,
but just is.

It is impossible to grasp facticity in its
brute nudity, since all that we will find of
it is already recovered and freely constructed.
The simple fact "of being there," at that
table, in that chair is already the pure object
of a limiting-concept and as such cannot be
grasped.[27]

In short, we can't think existence, but knowing that
we can't makes us aware that there is existence beyond
the reach of thought, and as Sartre goes on to show in
Nausea, while we can't think existence, we can experience it in moments of "nausea."

These then are some of the many interesting ways
in which thought can be described in terms of negation.
But there are positive ways as well. And of course
each of these negative ways can also be described
positively, as Sartre admits in discussing Heidegger's
positive characterization. And while it is true that
negation enters the world only with human thought,
so does being in the full sense of meaningful, understood being enter the world with and only with human
conceptualization. The for-itself is no less responsible for the phenomenon of being than it is for nothingness. Why the insistence, then, on the negative as

primary? Partly out of a sense of cleverness, perhaps,
a love of the paradoxical contrast of logical opposites
(e.g., "Being and Nothingness"). But it is also meant
to address itself to a long and honorable philosophical
tradition since Parmenides, and more recently enlivened
by Hegel, of whom Sartre's analysis is a deliberate
parody. This traditional interest in negation is of
paramount importance for our investigation of absurdity.

Recall our earlier remarks about Plato and Parmenides.
Nothing is first perceived as a direct contradiction of
Being. Since there is no nothing (this being a contradiction in terms), there can be nothing sensible to
say about it. Therefore, Parmenides argued, statements
about nonbeing (and indeed any negative statements)
are simply meaningless. Plato, finding this unacceptable, tried to translate nonbeing-statements (negative
statements) into positive statements about difference.
To say that Theaetetus is not tall is to say that he
falls within a different class of persons. But Plato's
analysis has extremely far reaching implications for the
theory of meaning, for it applies to the very nature of
assertions and not just to negative assertions. What
Plato has given us is nothing less than an analysis of
assertion. Paraphrased, Plato can be seen as saying that
to think is to think A of X and this is to think of X
as not being B, C or D.

So, "nothing" became associated first with difference
and then with assertion and finally with consciousness in
general as a kind of private, inner and silent assertion.
To describe something is to delimit its many possibilities.
Otherwise you haven't said anything. This is what under-
lies the problem of synthetic a priori knowledge, the
problem how to have significant, informative knowledge
with absolute certainty. Upon reflection, it looks like
we cannot have such a thing because to be absolutely
certain, the object of discussion must be as limited in
itself as our description of it, and this could only
result in trivial tautologies. To say anything significant is, be definition, to attribute to it one of many
possible properties. Thus the range of possibilities
for the object must always be larger than what you
attribute to it. But this is precisely what makes error
possible, that is, what you assert is possible but not
true turns out to be the case. So, significant certainty
turns out to be a contradiction in terms. Another way
of putting this is to say that just as the term "reality"
shows that there is more to existence than there is to

67

essence (that is, that the world transcends what we think
of it), so the term "nothing" shows that there is more to
essence than to existence (that imagination can outrun
the status quo). Horatio is right, there is more in
heaven and earth than is dreamed of in philosophy: but
the reverse holds. We can never equate the two in an
idealistic union.

This is the rich philosophical pedigree of the
concept "nothing," but of course "nothing" still retains
its ordinary, naive, gut-level sense of sheer void, so
that all these statements that "consciousness is nothing"
have the flavor of mystery and pardox, which appears to
be deliberate in Sartre, suggesting death, annihilation.
The terms Sartre uses are borrowed directly from Hegel.
In Hegel's famous analysis, Being (in-itself, or reality)
is the thesis; Nothing (for-itself, or consciousness)
is the antithesis' and Daseyn, or Determined Being (being
as, or conceived being) is their synthesis. Thus for
Hegel, as for Aristotle, being in the full sense is a
synthesis of essence and existence. For Sartre, however,
there is no synthesis of thought and reality, essence and
existence, and so the two remain deeply divided, as
Hartman points out.

It is the perception of this split that accounts for
the experience of absurdity and nausea. Being-in-itself
appears as totally alien to consciousness, a mere thing.
What we do understand of it turns out to be our own
descriptive concepts and labels.

Being is revealed as not being the for-itself...
It appears outside the for-itself, beyond all
reach, as that which determines the for-itself
in its being. But the fact of revealing being
as a totality does not touch being any more
than the fact of counting two cups on the table
touches the existence or nature of either of
them.[28]

The presence of for-itself to being reveals
being as a thing.[29]

Being is everywhere opposite me, around me;
it weighs down on me, it besieges me, and I
am perpetually referred from being to being;
that table which is there is being and nothing
more; that rock, that tree, that landscape --
being and nothing else. I want to grasp this

68

being and I no longer find anything but <u>myself</u>...
for in order to know being such as it is, it
would be necessary to be that being.[30]

Being is without reason, without cause, and
without necessity;... "there is" being
because the for-itself is such that there is
being.[31]

(That is, there is a concept of being only through human
thought; the concept of existence belongs to essence,
while existence itself transcends all concepts whatever.)

So, part of the experience of absurdity is the
experience of being as fundamentally alien from human
consciousness. As such being-in-itself is seen as
threatening and repugnant. In <u>Being and Nothingness</u> this
experience which Sartre calls "nausea" is limited to my
experience of my own body as an alien being-in-itself,
threatening, negating my self, my consciousness for-
itself. But it is threatening not only in the sense
that it reveals how I am not it, but in the more primitive sense described by Bertrand Russell in "A Free
Man's Worship" that I depend on this body, however
different I am from it internally, and that my very
being is at the mercy of something totally alien from
me. In <u>Nausea</u>, however, the sense of nausea is expanded
to include revulsion toward all physical objects divorced
from human content or meaning.

Despite the phenomenological style, there is an
unmistakable materialism in <u>Being and Nothingness</u>, a
kind of epiphenomenalism of the mind dependent on
material body of an alien nature, rising and falling
with it (which makes Sartre's later Marxism less difficult to reconcile with his earlier phenomenological
existentialism). We have already mentioned the weakness
of Sartre's attempted synthesis of these two different
types of being at the end of the book.

But after our description of the In-itself and
the For-itself, it appeared to us difficult
to establish a bond between them, we feared
that we might fall into an insurmountable
dualism.[32]

A well-founded fear. In a trivial sense Pan includes
both, just as "being" includes both if they are different sorts of being. But this is not enough for the kind
of synthesis Sartre needs. He needs to show that,
though different, each requires the other. And this

Sartre is not willing to admit. In direct opposition to
Hegel, Sartre argues that while being-for-itself depends
on being-in-itself, the reverse does not hold---being-
in-itself does not depend on being-for-itself. In his
famous argument about Classical and Romantic art, Hegel
assumes the reverse, that while you can't have a materia
form without spiritual content, you can have pure spiritual content without any material form. What this
amounts to is idealism. Sartre's position is the materialist converse of this.

> But although in one sense consciousness con-
> sidered in isolation is an abstraction, and
> although phenomena...are similarly abstract
> insofar as they cannot exist as phenomena
> without appearing to a consciousness, never-
> theless the being of phenomena as in an in-
> self which is what it is cannot be considered
> as an abstraction....Therefore while the
> relation of the for-itself to the in-itself
> is originally constitutive of the very being
> which is put into the relation, we should not
> understand that this relation is constitutive
> of the in-itself but rather of the for-
> itself.[33]

It is definitely a one-way street. Consciousness depend
on reality, but reality does not depend on consciousness
(only the intentional object depends on consciousness).
This makes a mockery of the synthesis of for-itself and
in-itself in the totality of Pan, as Sartre comes close
to admitting in one interesting passage.

> As for the totality of the for-itself and the
> in-itself, this has for its characteristic
> the fact that the for-itself makes itself
> other in relation to the in-itself but that
> the in-itself is in no way other than the
> for-itself in its being.[34]

It is this absolute division which is manifested in
the experience of absurdity. Not only an alien world,
but a world completely indifferent to any human conception or explanation. The world can literally do anything and we are conversely infinitely free.

Looking beyond the influence of Being and Nothingne
on Nausea to a more critical accounting, we must agree
with Camus that this total indifference is wildly
contrary to plain fact. Our explanations reflect to
some extent the limitations of the world on itself and

70

the world most certainly imposes many restrictions and limitations on my freedom to act in the world. (Indeed, this may be the only clear sense we have of "facticity".) The source of Sartre's enormous error would seem to be his confusion of the fact that consciousness and reality are different sorts of things, which they surely are, with the quite different claim that they therefore have no relation to one another. By the transcendence relation, reality can never be knowledge of reality. But that doesn't mean they can't be related in the knowledge relation. In thinking it is possible to understand an aspect of reality, and this is genuine, correctible knowledge of an alien reality, which can be progressively improved upon. As Camus points out, we can know reality; the only thing we cannot know is reality in itself. This confusion in Sartre's thinking is what leads, as Wild puts it, to

> the strange conception of the en soi...as
> an absolute plenum with no potency, and indeed
> no real relations to anything beyond....
> Heidegger suggests such a view by his con-
> ception of subhuman existence as a determinate
> being-on-hand..., something finished and simply
> there, in violent contrast to the unfinished
> potentiality of Dasein. In Sartre, this con-
> trast between a subhuman en soi that is fully
> in act, and a human pour soi...that is purely
> potential nothingness, is magnified to an
> exaggerated opposition that warps his whole
> ontology.[35]

Wild is right. Objects can't do just anything. Independently of all human interpretation, a piece of glass is more likely to break than a piece of rubber. There are limitations and some of these are reflected in thought (i.e., are understood by us). Recalling our discussion of the last chapter, it is ironic how much more sophisticated and incisive is Camus' position, though far less philosophical in style. As Hartmann points out,

> The same qualities do not appear everywhere.
> The availability of certain qualities and dis-
> crete units cannot be referred simply to our
> negation of being. Discreteness must somehow
> be grounded in being-in-itself.[36]

And as Hartmann argues, this problem is due to the lack of synthesis of the two terms which Sartre borrows from Hegel's opposition of Being and Nothing.

71

The opposition of subject and object in Sartre's
ontology coincides with the opposition at
the beginning of Hegel's _Logic_, but remains
arrested there.[37]

Sartre's ontology...is unable to account for
what there is per se from an objectively
ontological perspective, namely, individual
things and individual persons.[38]

Here, Sartre takes the side of Kantian realism against
Hegelian idealism, pushing Kant's position to an extreme. Thought converts pure existence into essence.
Kant and Sartre interpret this to mean that thought
thereby falsifies existence and that pure existence is
therefore always unknown (like Aristotle's matter).
Hegel interprets this same fact to mean that existence
is evolving into essence. We don't distort it; it
changes! Hence the idealist synthesis in Hegel which
Sartre, along with Kant, Locke and Aristotle, could not
find within a realist framework.

Nausea is the attempt to translate the metaphysics
of absurdity into human experience. Since we cannot
think existence we must locate it within some precogni-
tive experience. In the novel Sartre tries to show how
the world looks and feels to someone, namely Roquentin,
suffering "nausea," the concrete experience of absurdity.
The structure of the novel turns on the progressive dissolution of objects, as perceived by Roquentin and
systematically recorded daily in his diary, step by
step, from individual ordinary physical things to a
vast, all-encompassing emptiness. In the first stage
words become divorced from things which nonetheless
retain their discrete, distinct, individual, thingly
guise. In the second stage the lines of demarcation
between individual objects begin to dissolve and objects
melt together into a curious kind of fog. And finally,
in the third stage, this fog diffuses still further
into sheer emptiness, though this is only suggested
briefly at the very end of the novel. Within this
description of the perception of objects divorced from
meaning Sartre weaves the correlative notions, so
important in his later fiction, of freedom and adventure.

The manifest "story line" of the novel is very
thin. Antoine Roquentin's present stage of life comes
to an end as he abandons his two remaining illusions of
a meaningful existence--completing his historical research
on the 18th century figure, M. Rollebon, and recapturing

72

his sense of romantic adventure with his old lover,
Anny. The novel ends as Roquentin prepares to leave the
provincial capital, Bouville, where he had been living
the past few years, for Paris to begin a new life as a
fiction writer. The dominant themes of the novel
move on a very different plane, however, as Roquentin
records in painstaking detail a devastating change which
has occured in his experience of the world around him.

> I must tell how I see this table, this street,
> the people, packet of tobacco, since those
> are the things which have changed. I must
> determine the exact extent and nature of this
> change.[39]

It is a change of immense importance, yet words seem
incapable of describing it. Indeed, described in words,
there is no detectable change at all!

> For instance, here is a cardboard box holding
> my bottle of ink. I should try to tell how
> I saw it before and now how I [do]. Well,
> it's a parallelopiped rectangle, it opens--
> that's stupid, there's nothing I can say about
> it.[40]

It is not Roquentin who has changed but, somehow, the
objects themselves. Whatever change has occured in
Roquentin's outlook must indeed be explained in terms
of the changed status of objects in the world.

> The Nausea is not inside me: I feel it out
> there in the wall, in the suspenders, every-
> where around me. It makes itself one with the
> cafe, I am the one who is within it.[41]

Roquentin then begins describing a series of experiences with particular, everyday physical objects in
which the disturbing quality of these objects gradually
emerges. At first, in the case of the stone on the
beach, it is a very confused experience, difficult to
understand and describe.

> I saw something which disgusted me, but I no
> longer know whether it was the sea or the
> stone. The stone was flat and dry, especially
> on one side, damp and muddy on the other. I
> held it by the edges with my fingers wide
> apart so as not to get them dirty....[42]

Later, with the glass of beer, it becomes clearer

to Roquentin that the difficulty in putting into words
what he is trying to describe is precisely that it is
something beyond words and distinct from linguistic
description

> Everywhere, now, there are objects like this
> glass of beer on the table there. When I
> see it, I feel like saying: "Enough."...
> I have been avoiding looking at this glass
> of beer....I don't want to see it...."Well,
> what's the matter with that glass of beer?"
> It's just like all the others. It's bevelled
> on the edges, has a handle,...I know all
> that, but I know there is something else.
> Almost nothing. But I can't explain what I
> see. [43]

It is not, of course, the objects themselves which
have literally changed, but like the absurd experience
generally, the semantical relation of words to objects.
Words can only describe how one glass of beer is like
other glasses of beer, i.e., what they share in common,
bevelled edges, handle, etc.--the universal essence of
"a glass of beer." Words are in principle, then,
incapable of describing the individual existence of
this particular glass of beer. Of all the things we
feel it is difficult to put into words, existence is
the one thing, and indeed the only thing, where this
is literally impossible.

In our ordinary experience we look at the existing
object in terms of its essence, we see that as a
glass of beer, one among many, an instance of its
"type," and thus "avoid" looking at this glass of beer.
We see the essence in the existing individual, we do
not see its existence, that is, we do not see it as
the unique individual it is. "Everything is what it
is and not another thing," as Joseph Butler once
remarked, but we don't see things this way: we see them
as something other than themselves, as glasses, stones,
etc. We think we have been looking at the individual
object, while all along we have seen only its general
identity or essence. This is the basis of Roger Fry's
distinction in Vision and Design between seeing things
in ordinary perception and looking at them in an
aesthetic context.

> The needs of our actual life are so imperative,
> that the sense of vision becomes highly specialised
> in their service. With an admirable economy we

74

learn to see only so much as is needful for
our purposes; but this is in fact very little,
just enough to recognize and identify each
object or person; that done, they go into
an entry in our mental catalogue and are no
more really seen. In actual life the normal
person really only reads the labels as it were
on the objects around him and troubles no
further....It is only when an object exists
in our lives for no other purpose than to be
seen that we really look at it....Biologically
speaking, art is a blasphemy. We were given
our eyes to see things, not to look at them.
Life takes care that we all learn the lesson
thoroughly, so that at a very early age we
have acquired a very considerable ignorance of
visual appearances....The subtlest differences
of appearance that have a utility value still
continue to be appreciated, while large and
important visual characters, provided they are
useless for life, will pass unnoticed....
Children have not learned it fully, and so
they look at things with some passion. Even
the grown man keeps something of his unbio-
logical, disinterested vision with regard to a
few things. He still looks at flowers, and
does not merely see them....The vision with
which we regard such objects is quite distinct
from the practical vision of our instinctive
life. In the practical vision we have no more
concern after we have read the label on the
object; vision ceases the moment it has
served its biological function.

But this begins to make clearer the disturbing
aspect of objects as mere objects. As a glass of beer,
or a piece of writing paper, objects are assigned useful purposes and so occupy a friendly place in the world
of our common needs and interests. In his popular
radio broadcast just after the war, later published as
"Existenialism and Humanism," Sartre makes clear the
functionalist, purposive nature of the human perception
of the essence of an object.

If one considers an article of manufacture--as,
for example, a book or a paper-knife--one
sees that it has been made by an artisan who
had a conception of it...and...pre-existent
technique of production which is a part of that
conception and is, at bottom, a formula. Thus
the paper-knife is at the same time an article

75

producible in a certain manner and one which,
on the other hand, serves a definite purpose,
for one cannot suppose that a man would produce
a paper-knife without knowing what it was
for. Let us say, then, of the paper-knife
that its essence--that is to say the sum of
the formulae and the qualities which made its
production and its definition possible--
precedes existence.... [44]

In this same article Sartre tries to show how we
extend this functionalist way of understanding objects
to nonmanufactured objects, and indeed to everything
we come in contact with. "Here, then, we are viewing
the world from a technical standpoint...When we think of
God as the creator, we are thinking of him...as a supernatural artisan," [45] an idea first expressed in Plato's
Timaeus. As an example of this extension of purposeful explanation, whose overtness strikes us as cute, or
clever, consider the kind of children's book which
begins: "The cow is there to give us milk; the hen is
there to give us eggs; the pig is there to give us
bacon," in which the world's resistance to purposeful
rendering, especially in the last case, is conveniently
glossed over. Stripped of their familiar role, objects
become mere things totally indifferent to our purposes
and existing as limits to our freedom to act purposefully.

But if the mere thinghood of the object, its
existence, is necessarily beyond words, how does Sartre,
or Roquentin, describe it in the novel? This poses a
very serious problem. After we have kicked or pounded
the object, or repeated emphatically, "it just is!",
what is there to say about existence? Perhaps we should
simply remain silent. Sartre's solution is to describe
the object in terms other than its customary utilitarian, functional description. He does not refuse to
describe the object entirely, but simply in its most
customary fashion. The streetcar seat is described, for
example, as the body of a dead bloated donkey floating
down the river and its rough knap as the claws of tiny
animals. This device resembles poetic imagery in which
we are invited to see familiar objects in unfamiliar
ways. Insofar as we find this possible we are tacitly
being persuaded that the object is not tied exclusively
to any one description, thus loosening, however slightly,
that naive link between word and object. These alternative descriptions provide a sense of the object transcending its usual description, and thereby, an indirect
sense of its existence transcending all description.

Obviously words cannot describe what lies beyond words, but there are uses of words which can suggest indirectly a nonsemantical reality. In Being and Nothingness this nonsemantical reality is referred to as the "being of phenomena" which does not enter into any internal "relationships," a "being-in-itself" which just is--an interesting use of words to refer to what cannot be verbally described. So in Nausea the object beyond all description is nonetheless described though in unusual, metaphorical ways, and from unusual points of view.

> Today, I was watching the riding boots of a
> cavalry officer who was leaving his barracks.
> As I followed them with my eyes, I saw a
> piece of paper lying beside a puddle. I
> thought the officer was going to crush the
> paper into the mud with his heel, but no:
> he straddled paper and puddle in a single
> step. I went up to it: it was a lined page,
> undoubtedly torn from a school notebook. The
> rain had drenched and twisted it, it was
> covered with blisters and swellings like a
> burned hand; the red line of the margin was
> smeared into a pink splotch; ink had run in
> places. The bottom of the page disappeared
> beneath a crust of mud. I bent down, already
> rejoicing at the touch of this pulp, fresh
> and tender, which I should roll in my fingers
> into greyish balls. I was unable...Objects
> should not touch because they are not alive.
> You use them, put them back in place, you
> live among them: they are useful, nothing
> more. But they touch me, it is unbearable.
> I am afraid of being in contact with them as
> though they were living beasts.[46]

Of course, inanimate objects are not living animals, but this metaphor, this way of seeing them does bring out their indifference to us, the separate "lives" they lead once they have been removed from the perspective of their utility to us as human beings. Nor is a streetcar seat a dead animal, though this too serves to evoke the sense of a physical reality completely untouched by the animating spirit of human consciousness, a dull, leaden material existence heavy as a corpse. Since sight and hearing are the most intellectual and hence semantically linked senses, it is primarily through touch that Roquentin becomes aware of the brute existence of things. We see them in terms of their generalized significance or identity; but when we feel them we sense that there is more to an

77

object than the label by which we classify it.

> Suddenly, there it is: the Nausea....My
> hand is clutching the handle of the dessert
> knife. I feel this black wooden handle. My
> hand holds it. My hand. Personally, I would
> rather let this knife alone: what good is it
> to be always touching something? Objects are
> not made to be touched. It is better to
> slip between them, avoiding them as much as
> possible....[47]

Included among the objects thus divorced, alienated
from descriptive, semantic meaning is Roquentin's own
body and the parts of his body. In Being and Nothingness this is the entire focus of nausea, while in
Nausea it is only a part, though a significant part of
that experience.

> I see my hand spread out on the table. It
> lives--it is me. It opens, the fingers open
> and point. It is lying on its back. It
> shows me its fat belly. It looks like an
> animal turned upside down. The fingers are
> the paws.[48]

Similarly on the streetcar seat, it is touch which
reveals the thing qua thing, which in transcending the
utilitarian identity of the object appears as a
thing with a will of its own, opposing mine, like an
animal.

> I lean my hand on the seat but pull it back
> hurriedly; it exists. This thing I'm sitting
> on, leaning my hand on, is called a seat.
> They made it purposively for people to sit
> on, they took leather, springs and cloth,
> they went to work with the idea of making
> a seat and when they finished, that was what
> they had made. They carried it here, into this
> car and the car is now rolling and jolting
> with its rattling windows, carrying this red
> thing in its bosom. I murmur: 'It's a seat,'
> a little like an exorcism. But the word
> stays on my lips: it refuses to go and put
> itself on the thing. It stays what it is,
> with its red plush, thousands of little red
> paws in the air, all still, little dead paws.
> This enormous belly turned upward, bleeding,
> inflated--bloated with all its dead paws, this

belly floating in this car, in this grey
sky, is not a seat. It could just as well
be a dead donkey tossed about in the water,
floating with the current, belly in the air
in a great grey river, a river of floods; and
I could be sitting on the donkey's belly, my
feet dangling in the clear water. Things are
divorced from their names. They are there,
grotesque, headstrong, gigantic and it seems
ridiculous to call them seats or say anything
at all about them: I am in the midst of
things, nameless things. Alone, without
words, defenseless, they surround me, are
beneath me, behind me, above me. They demand
nothing, they don't impose themselves: they
are there.[49]

The object is now divorced entirely from its name,
and from all human words, concepts and descriptions. As
such it is essentially indifferent to linguistic description; it could be described as anything.

I was in the park just now. The roots of the
chestnut tree were sunk in the ground just
under my bench. I couldn't remember it was
a root any more. The words had vanished and
with them the significance of things, their
methods of use, and the feeble points of
reference which men have traced on their
surface. I was sitting, stooping forward,
head bowed, alone in front of this black,
knotty mass, entirely beastly, which fright-
ened me.[50]

And even whole streets.

I know it's the Rue Boulibet but I don't
recognize it. Usually, when I start down it
I seem to cross a deep layer of good sense:
squat and awkward, the Rue Boulibet, with its
tarred and uneven surface, looked like a
national highway when it passes through rich
country towns with solid, three-story houses
for more than half a mile; I called it a
country road and it enchanted me because it
was so out of place, so paradoxical in a
commercial port. Today the houses are there
but they have lost their rural look: they
are buildings and nothing more.[51]

In our ordinary experience words and object are

joined together into an indistinguishable unity. In
the nauseous experience of absurdity, on the other hand,
the two split apart. This creates a change in the
object; it also creates a change in the word. We say,
for example, that an object is black, and "black" looks
like the name of a distinct quality, just as "seat"
looks like the name of a distinct object. But, of
course, black, is only a generalized kind of quality,
applying to many different sorts and degrees of black.
Just as objects become mere objects in the experience
of absurdity, so do words become mere words, that is,
mere sounds and marks detached from their meaningful
connection to the world.

> Black? I felt the word deflating, emptied of
> meaning with extraordinary rapidity. Black?
> The root was not black, there was no black
> on this piece of wood--there was...something
> else: black...did not exist. I looked at
> the root: was it more than black or almost
> black? But I soon stopped questioning myself
> because...I had already felt their cold,
> inert qualities elude me, slip through my
> fingers. [52]

How can a black root not be black? How can a
seat not be a seat? The point concerns the semantical
relation telescoped in the little word "is" in "is
black" and "is a seat." In the sense in which this
relation is understood to name distinct ontological
entities (whether objects or qualities) the relation
does not hold and in that sense the object is not black
or a seat. But of course in the sense in which this
particular object and quality are classifiable within th
broad abstract concept of "seat" and "black," it is a
seat and is black. The main thing is to see that black
is not an objective entity ("black did not exist"),
but only a humanly constructed essence or label. In
the experience of nausea, objects refuse to accept their
labels, and labels refuse to attach themselves to
objects. Detached from one another both word and object
take on a disturbing strangeness. In a more playful
way, children will similarly disassociate word from
object by repeating a word over and over again until its
"existence" as a mere sound is detached from its meaning, and it begins to sound funny.

Names for the qualities of objects are therefore
in precisely the same fix as names for the objects themselves, mere idealized abstractions, not proper names of
any actual existence.

80

The sounds, smells, the tastes. When they ran
quickly under your nose like startled hares and
you didn't pay too much attention, you might
believe them to be simple and reassuring,
you might believe that there was real blue in
the world, real red, a real perfume of almonds
or violets. But as soon as you held on to
them for an instant, this feeling of comfort
and security gave way to a deep uneasiness:
colours, tastes, and smells were never real,
never themselves and nothing but themselves....
[The black] looked like a colour, but also
...like a bruise or a secretion, like an
oozing--and something else, an odour, for
example, it melted into the odour of wet
earth, warm, moist wood, into a black odour
that spread like varnish over this sensitive
wood, in a flavour of chewed, sweet fibre....
But this richness was lost in confusion and
finally was no more because it was too much.[53]

As Bergson points out, it is the very nature of
conceptual, semantical understanding of an object to
break it up into discrete, namable units, even though
the object itself is not so sharply divisible. Linguistically and conceptually even the color spectrum
is composed of discrete, individual colors, even though,
as a continuum, the spectrum is not, by definition, so
divisible.

Our mind, which seeks for solid points of
support, has for its main function in the ordinary course of life that of representing
states and things. It takes, at long
intervals, almost instantaneous views of the
undivided mobility of the real. It thus
obtains sensations and ideas. In this way
it substitutes for the continuous the dis-
continuous, for motion stability, for tendency
in the process of change, fixed points marking
a direction of change and tendency. This
substitution is necessary...to positive
science.[54]

And, he might have added, necessary for all ordinary
understanding and discourse. One of the ways in which
poetry differs from prose is its device of mixing
descriptions which ordinarily belong to different sense
modalities (called syncretism) in a way which calls to
mind the preconceptual experience of a more homo-
geneous, continuous world, a world in which, as in

Sartre's example, we see the moisture, warmth, earthy smell of the tree root.

If words do not attach essentially to objects but are imposed from without by men, then objects can be described as anything. But if so, then, so far as we know, objects can be anything. Hence, the all-pervasive contingency of physical existence. The reasons, explanations we offer in order to relate objects together into a pattern of systematic understanding, whether in science or common sense, are, just like the words we use, mere human projections. The experience of nausea is the realization that all words, descriptions and explanations are merely human constructs which have nothing whatever to do with real existence, though they serve a valuable utilitarian function. In this sense the two divided realms of thought and object (being-for-itself and being-in-itself, essence and existence) are completely free from one another. Objects are free from our labels and we are free, as thinking beings, from objects. However we interpret the world the world remains what it is; and no interpretation of objects can determine that which is interpreting them (human thought since the interpretation (essence) must spring from the interpreter (human existence). In this one case, and only in this case, existence precedes essence. In order for the world to have any influence on me, it must be related to me. But relations exist only in human thought, not in reality. Therefore, sociological, psychological and physical determinism are merely theories As such they are determined by me; I am not determined by them. The result is a world of total freedom.

> I understood the Nausea,...I did not formulate
> my discoveries to myself. But I think it
> would be easy for me to put them in words
> now. The essential thing is contingency. I
> mean that one cannot define existence as
> necessity. To exist is simply to be there
> ....Contingency is not a delusion, a probability
> which can be dissipated; it is the absolute....
> All is free, this park, this city and myself.[55]

As a result, anything can happen.

> What is something were to happen? What if some-
> thing suddenly started throbbing? Then they
> would notice it was there and they'd think
> their hearts were going to burst....For
> example, the father of a family might go out

82

for a walk, and, across the street, he'll
see something like a red rag, blown towards him
by the wind. And when the rag has gotten
close to him he'll see that it is a crawling,
skipping, a piece of writhing flesh rolling
in the gutter, spasmodically shooting out
spurts of blood.[56]

Since objects cannot be in any way related to one
another they can only be conceived as atomistic.

We were a heap of living creatures, irritated,
embarrassed at ourselves, we hadn't the slightest reason to be there, none of us, each one,
confused, vaguely alarmed, felt in the way in
relation to the others. In the way: it was
the only relationship I could establish
between these trees, these gates, these
stones. In vain I tried to count the chestnut trees, to locate them by their relationship to the Velleda, to compare their height
with the height of the plane trees: each of
them escaped the relationship in which I
tried to enclose it, isolated itself, and
overflowed. Of these relations (which I
insisted on maintaining in order to delay the
crumbling of the human world, measures,
quantitites, and directions)--I felt myself
to be the arbitrator; they no longer had their
teeth into things.[57]

Things are always more than the names, descriptions,
and relations in terms of which we try to fix them in
the orbit of our human concerns. The world transcends
and overflows any human understanding of it. The irony
is that we can experience reality, being-in-itself,
but cannot describe it in any way whatever. Even words
like "reality," "being," "existence" and "nothingness"
can do no more than express the feeling, or experience of
nausea and how it differs from our ordinary experience
of the world. It cannot describe a world beyond description. As Sartre makes clear in Being and Nothingness,
even nothingness is a human concept which comes into
the world with and only with human thought. In Nausea
this is translated into Roquentin's experience of absurdity.

I knew it was the World, the naked World suddenly revealing itself, and I choked with
rage at this gross, absurd being. You couldn't
even wonder where all that sprang from, or how

83

it was that a world came into existence,
rather than nothingness. It didn't make
sense, the World was everywhere....There had
been nothing <u>before</u> it. Nothing. There had
never been a moment in which it could not have
existed. That was what worried me: of course
there was no reason for this flowing larva
to exist. But it was impossible for it not
to exist. It was unthinkable: to imagine
nothingness you had to be there already,
in the midst of the World, eyes wide open
and alive; nothingness was only an idea in
my head....This nothingness had not come
<u>before</u> existence, it was an existence like
any other and appeared after many others.[58]

The same absurd thought-object gap applies equally
to any historical explanation of the world, in particular to Roquentin's historical account of Rollebon.
Roquentin now sees that here too nothing can be veri-
fied; it is all a matter of subjective projection.

I am beginning to believe that nothing can
ever be proved. These are honest hypotheses
which take the facts into account: but I
sense so definitely that they come from me,
and that they are simply a way of unifying
my own knowledge....Slow, lazy, sulky, the
facts adapt themselves to the rigour of the
order I wish to give them; but it remains
outside of them. I have the feeling of doing
a work of pure imagination.[59]

This is more apparent in the case of those things
we use as historical evidence for our hypotheses.
Roquentin is examining a letter actually written by
Rollebon. As evidence this object links Roquentin to
Rollebon and the past in an elaborate interconnected
web connecting this piece of evidence to thousands of
others. But it exists as evidence only within a human
point of view, a historical perspective concerned with
the past. In itself, it is just a piece of paper with
dried ink marks on it. It is only within the human
gaze that it can mean something more. As people we can
make it mean more by projecting our historical concerns
upon it, but in itself it is just a thing--not even a
thing from the past, but a thing existing <u>now</u>, sitting
there on Roquentin's desk. In copying out a particular
sentence from the letter, the whole elaborately construc

84

facade of history collapses before Roquentin's eyes.

> "Care had been taken to spread the most sinis-
> ter rumours..." I had thought out this sent-
> ence, at first it had been a small part of
> myself. Now it was inscribed on the paper, it
> took sides against me. I didn't recognize it
> any more....It was there, in front of me;
> in vain for me to trace some sign of its
> origin....I looked anxiously around me: the
> present, nothing but the present....The true
> nature of the present revealed itself:
> it was what exists, and all that was not
> present did not exist. The past did not
> exist. Not at all. Not in things, not even
> in my thoughts....Now I knew: things are
> entirely what they appear to be--and behind
> them....There is nothing.[60]

As we pointed out in our analysis of Sartre's
conception of human thought in terms of "nothing,"
whatever depth or meaning the world has is creatively
achieved by connecting what actually exists here and
now with what does not exist, but is expected to do so
or can be made to do so through human agency. Here
Sartre has exerted enormous influence on the New
Realists, like Robbe-Grillet, who try to remove all
human interpretation from description and present the
flat, unemotional surface of existence. The sense of
the historical past is simply the most vivid illustration of this distinction of "manifest-latent"
content. Rollebon doesn't exist, nor indeed any of the
past except as a current interest in our minds today.

> I had said that the past did not exist. And
> suddenly, noiseless, M. de Rollebon had returned
> to his nothingness. I held his letters in
> my hands,...He is the one, I said,...who made
> these marks....too late: these words had no
> more sense. Nothing existed but a bundle of
> yellow pages.[61]

So, too, with the idea of romantic adventure in
life which Roquentin had been hoping in vain to recapture in his relationship with Anny. When he finally
meets Anny, after a long separation, he discovers that
she has given up completely the search for a sense of
adventure and is now quite content to merely exist--
like a pet animal, eating, sleeping, and passively
enjoying whatever of life's pleasures happen to come

85

along. He also discovers that the old adventure with
Anny had been deliberately constructed by Anny, like a
work of art. Now Roquentin comes to see that there is
no adventure in reality; adventure is nothing more than
a human decision to dramatically link up events in our
own minds. The events themselves have nothing to do
with one another, certainly nothing dramatic or adven-
turous.

> This feeling of adventure definitely does not
> come from events.... It's rather the way in
> which the moments are linked together...You
> suddenly feel that time is passing, that each
> instant leads to another, this one to another
> one, and so on: that each instant is annih-
> ilated, and that it isn't worth while to
> hold it back, etc., etc. And then you attri-
> bute this property to events which appear to
> you in the instants; what belongs to the form
> you carry over to the content. [62]

The experience of nausea is unusual because of a
constant pressure of normalcy against it, the pressure t
see the world in terms of our meanings, explanations
and purposes. Absurdity appears for a moment and then
is as quickly gone, replaced by the mundane, friendly
ordinary vision of the world.

> But suddenly it became impossible for me to
> think of the existence of the root. It was
> wiped out, I could repeat in vain: it exists,
> it is still there..., it no longer meant
> anything. Existence is not something which
> lets being thought of from a distance; it
> must invade you suddenly, master you, weigh
> heavily on your heart like a great motionless
> beast--or else there is nothing more at all....
> Suddenly they existed, then suddenly they
> existed no longer: existence is without
> memory; of the vanished it retains nothing--
> not even a memory. [63]

The experience of existence must be prelinguistic,
preconceptual, visceral, and, since it is by definition
beyond words and concepts, it is also beyond the reach
of memory. It is a total assault on the person, an
all-or-nothing proposition.

> I realized that there was no half-way house
> between non-existence and this flaunting abun-
> dance. If you existed, you had to exist _all_

the way, as far as mouldiness, bloatedness, obscenity were concerned.[64]

Either we feel raw existence, that is, in Sartre's language, either we "exist," or else we sink back into words, concepts, into essence. Since the two are absolutely opposite, we cannot do both at once.

> There was so much, tons and tons of existence, endless: I stifled at the depths of this immense weariness. And then suddenly the park emptied as through a great hole, the World disappeared as it had come, or else I woke up-- in any case, I saw no more of it; nothing was left but the yellow earth around me, out of which dead branches rose upward. I got up and went out. Once at the gate, I turned back. Then the garden smiled at me. I leaned against the gate and watched for a long time. The smile of the trees, of the laurel, meant something.[65]

Throughout the novel, Roquentin's experience of absurdity becomes more frequent and prolonged and more and more encompassing. Roquentin's attitude toward the nausea experience is also increasingly ambivalent. Nausea is the understanding of bare existence, and to understand this is to truly "exist" as a human being. On the one hand this frees us from the illusions, naivete, and pretense of ordinary experience, but on the other hand it is a revolting, disgusting experience. There is an ambiguous envy in Roquentin's attitude toward those who remain within the blissful ignorance of the mundane outlook, comfortably projecting meaning onto the world, unaware that they are doing so.

> Each one of them has his little personal difficulty which keeps him from noticing that he exists.[66]

> I would so like to let myself go, forget myself, sleep. But I can't, I'm suffocating: existence penetrates me everywhere, through the eyes, the nose, the mouth...And suddenly, suddenly, the veil is torn away, I have understood, I have seen...[67]

By seeing existence through the eyes of essence, ordinary people do not "exist," that is, do not confront pure existence face to face as Roquentin does, and it is this fascination with the "naked World" which draws Roquentin farther and farther into "the Nausea."

Never, until these last few days, had I understood the meaning of 'existence.' I was like
the others...I said, like them, 'The ocean is
green; that white speck up there is a seagull,'
but I didn't feel that it existed...; usually
existence hides itself. It is there, around
us, in us, it is us, you can't say two words
without mentioning it, but you can never
touch it. When I believed I was thinking
about it, I must believe that I was thinking
nothing, my head was empty, or there was just
one word in my head, the word 'to be.' Or
else I was thinking of belonging, I was telling
myself that the sea belonged to the class of
green objects, or that the green was a part of
the quality of the sea. Even when I looked
at things, I was miles from dreaming that they
existed: they looked like scenery to me...,
they served me as tools, I foresaw their resistance....If anyone had asked me what existence was, I would have answered, in good
faith, that it was nothing, simply an empty
form which was added to external things without changing anything to their nature. And
then all of a sudden, there it was, clear as
day: existence had suddenly unveiled itself.
It had lost the harmless look of an abstract
category: it was the very paste of things...
the root, the park gates, the bench,...all
that had vanished: the diversity of things,
their individuality, were only an appearance,
a veneer. This veneer had melted leaving
soft, monstrous masses, all in disorder,--
naked, in a frightful, obscene nakedness.68

In this last passage we see the first sign of the
curious transformation of heavy and dense, proliferating
absurd matter into a soft, melting mush, or, the
symbol in Nausea, fog. If words are divorced from objec
the objects can be described as anything. But if so,
then they can be anything, so far as we know. But if
they can be anything, then they are nothing definite.
Without human consciousness there are no lines of
demarcation between objects, and without lines of demarcation there are no divisions distinguishing one
object from another. And so their overt heaviness
dissolves into the lightness described by Ionesco
which we referred to at the outset. What is peculiar
in Sartre's treatment is the imposition of an intermediary fog or soup between the extremes of heavy, atomistic, mere things and pure emptiness which we find in

Beckett and the later Ionesco.

> Fog had filled the room: not the real fog,
> that had gone a long time ago--but the other,
> the one the streets were still full of, which
> came out of the walls and pavements. The
> inconsistency of inanimate objects! The
> books were still there, arranged in alpha-
> betical order on the shelves with their
> brown and black backs and their labels....
> But...how can I explain it? Usually, power-
> ful and squat, along with the stove, the green
> lamps, the wide windows, the ladders, they dam
> up the future. As long as you stay between
> these walls, whatever happens must happen on
> the right or the left of the stove....Thus
> these objects serve at least to fix the limits
> of probability. Today they fixed nothing at
> all: it seemed that their very existence was
> subject to doubt, that they had the greatest
> difficulty in passing from one instant to
> the next. I held the book I was reading
> tightly in my hands: but the most violent
> sensations went dead. Nothing seemed true; I
> felt surrounded by cardboard scenery which
> could quickly be removed. The world was
> waiting, holding its breath, making itself
> small--it was waiting for its convulsion, its
> Nausea,...I murmured: _Anything_ can happen,
> _anything_. [69]

> _They_ _did_ _not_ _want_ to exist, only they could not
> help themselves. So they quietly minded their
> own business; the sap rose up slowly through the
> structure, half reluctant and the roots sank
> slowly into the earth. But at each instant
> they seemed on the verge of leaving every-
> thing there and obliterating themselves. [70]

Much of this can be articulated, I think, in terms
of dialectical stages in the order of our learning
process. At first the cognitive identity of individual
objects becomes detached, but the objects still exist
as distinct entities and their spatial and temporal
relations still hold the world together as a rational,
if somewhat abstract, system of spatio-temporal relationships of physical objects. But, of course, this is
only the thin edge of the wedge. As Kant pointed out
several centuries earlier, even to think of things as
objects, and to relate them together spatially and

temporally is no less a human achievement and a human imposition than the acts of labelling and classifying. This is Borges' thesis in his "New Refutation of Time" referred to in the first chapter. Aspects of the world are not themselves related into semi-permanent objects, but it is we who create these relationships. Similarly, objects are not themselves related to one another spatially or temporally, but it is we who assign these relationships to them for our own human purposes in making the world a more familiar and manageable place. Thus we realize that space, time and objecthood are human projections upon the world and that reality is something other than this, and, as these relationships cease to apply, objects begin to melt and dissolve into a soft, amorphous jelly.

It is through the extreme separation of thought and existence, ironically, that Roquentin finds a kind of solution to the problem of absurdity at the end of the novel by renouncing existence and embracing the world of pure essence as his only refuge. The problem with absurdity is the distance between things and our descriptions of them. But as Descartes discovered, this distance cannot touch pure thought, or purely cultural objects, such as circles, songs, and fictional stories. These "objects" only exist in description, so there is no gap in their case between description and object, and hence no absurdity.

This notion first appears in the contrast of a circle with the exposed root of the chestnut tree.

> Absurd, irreducible; nothing--not even a
> profound, secret upheaval of nature--could
> explain it...neither ignorance nor knowledge
> was important: the world of explanations
> and reasons is not the world of existence....
> A circle is not absurd, it is clearly ex-
> plained by the rotation of a straight segment
> around one of its extremities. But neither
> does a circle exist. This root, on the other
> hand, existed in such a way that I could not
> explain it. Knotty, inert, nameless,...
> in vain to repeat: "This is a root"--it
> didn't work any more. I saw clearly that you
> could not pass from its function as a root, as
> a breathing pump, to that, to this hard and
> compact skin of a sea lion, to this oily,
> callous, headstrong look. The function explained
> nothing: it allowed you to understand

generally that it was a root, but not _that_ one at all.[71]

In the language of Being and Nothingness, the circle belongs to the human world of being-for-itself, while the tree root belongs to the nonhuman world of being-in-itself. Hence between the root and our human, functionalist account of it there is always a gap which thought can never fill, a gap which doesn't occur in the case of the circle since both the circle and our explanation of it occupy the same thought side of the great divide between thought and object. As Plato first pointed out in his account of the divided line in The Republic, when we transcribe an ideal object onto paper we never equate the marks on paper with the object to which those marks refer. The circle drawn on the blackboard is not "the circle." Numerals are not numbers, etc. There are many objects of human culture which we recognize _through_ physical objects whose existence nonetheless transcends those physical objects. Poems, novels, music do not exist entirely in the pages on which they are printed.

In examining Rollebon's sentence Roquentin realized that the historical meaning can only exist in the mind, in an activity of mind Sartre later termed the unrealizing function of mind. A person who couldn't unrealize, that is, one who saw physical marks on paper _only_ as physical marks on paper could never see a piece of paper _as_ a description of a historical event, or _as_ a drawing of a ship at sea, or _as_ a poem about a lost love.

Similarly in the case of music. The existence of the music cannot be identified completely with any physical object, such as a score, or a phonograph record. In one of Sartre's most intriguing examples Roquentin contemplates an old jazz recording of "Some of These Days". Like circles, the song doesn't "exist"--that is, does not exist over and above human interpretive thought.

It does not exist...if I were to get up and rip this record from the table which holds it, if I were to break it in two, I wouldn't reach it. It is beyond--always beyond something, a voice, a violin note. Through layers and layers of existence, it veils itself, thin and firm, and when you want to seize it, you find only exist- ants, you butt against existants devoid of sense. It is behind them; I don't even hear it, I hear sounds, vibrations in the air which unveil it.

91

It does not exist because it has nothing superfluous: it is all the rest in relation to it
which is superfluous. It is.[72]

If the tree root is in itself pure existence, then the
music in itself is pure essence. It does not "exist";
it "is". And in the same sense Roquentin says, in the
following sentence, "And I, too, wanted to be". Just as
we can "exist" in absurd awareness of existence, so we
can "be" in an ideal world of pure essence. Renouncing
both naive absorption in the world and the "existence" of
nausea, Roquentin here turns his back on objective reali
in favor of a world of pure thought which absurdity cannot touch.

    Thus, in the end, instead of renouncing writing
altogether, Roquentin gives up historical writing for
fiction as the ideal escape from physical existence.
Unlike the historians, who pretend to be writing about
the real world, things as they really happened in the
past, the fiction writer cuts all ties with the existing world in favor of a world within his own mind.
Unlike the historian, therefore, the fiction writer
frees himself from the absurd gap between description an
reality, essence and existence. It is senseless to try
to corroborate a fictional account with reality because
fiction doesn't refer to any actual reality. As Rilke
urges in Duino Elegies, if we cannot return to a humanly
interpreted world in which we see physical reality
through human eyes, then it is better to turn to objects
of pure thought. If we can no longer achieve the essenc
existence synthesis, we had better strive for essence
alone. At least this beats nausea.

    Another type of book, I don't quite know which
    kind--but you would have to guess, behind the
    printed words, behind the pages, at something
    which would not exist, which would be above
    existence. A story, for example, something
    that could never happen, an adventure. It
    would have to be beautiful and hard as steel
    to make people ashamed of their existence.[73]

If this sounds like idealism, which it surely does, we
are brought back to our initial dichotomy--either
dualism or idealism, there is no resolution of this
dilemma in Sartre.

    Of course, Sartre's position is not really ideal-
istic since the ideal world into which he retreats is st

92

contrasted with the real world of sheer existence (which the idealist would not countenance). But can he, or anyone, reject existence in favor of a world of pure essence? Only if the two are as utterly distinct as Sartre contends they are. But, as Camus shows us very clearly they are not absolutely separated from one another. Though none of our interpretations match reality completely or exactly, some obviously come closer than others. For all its admitted inadequacy, to describe a seat as a seat is better than describing it as a sunflower. Words are not the same as objects, but they can describe objects, and though words can never describe objects completely, or exhaustively, they can be relatively successful. Nor is fiction entirely removed from the ordinary world of existence. A story is constructed of elements (people, cities, streets, rivers, beer glasses, etc.) lifted out of a context of real existence, and the mood or theme of the story reflects back on that real world from which those elements were borrowed. The story of the wicked witch, for example, is based on the idea children already have of old women in the real world, and may in turn create a negative bias in the child's mind against those elderly women he comes in contact with in everyday life.

It is interesting that the succeeding generation of writers who were greatly influenced by Sartre, such as Robbe-Grillet and Butor, criticize Sartre, not for his misguided attempt to describe reality stripped of all human meaning, but for his (and Camus') failure to provide this neutral description. Thus the New Novelists press on toward what I have argued is the illusory goal of a neutral description of the thing-in-itself, pure existence stripped of all essence.

Robbe-Grillet, for example, holds that while all previous writers believe they are realists, none of them actually are. All so-called realism is simply a form on anthropomorphism. Old forms of writing seem unrealistic simply because we have become familiar with their stylistic conventions and thus aware of them as conventional, and hence as unrealistic. New forms of writing appear realistic because they abandon these tired, worn-out conventions which we recognize as conventional in favor of conventions which are too new to be recognized as conventional. Later, of course, the new conventions loose their transparancy and we see them for what they are--conventions, not reality. We will see this theme of alternating transparancy and opaqueness of stylistic conventions developed in Ionesco and Beckett.

> All writers believe they are realists...
> All of them are right...each one has
> different ideas about reality...It is
> easy, moreover, to understand why literary
> revolutions have always been made in the
> name of realism. When a form of writing
> has lost its initial vitality..., when it
> has become a vulgar recipe, an academic
> mannerism which its followers respect only out
> of routine or laziness, without ever question-
> ing its necessity, then it is indeed a return
> to the real which constitutes the arraignment
> of the dead formulas and the search for new
> forms capable of continuing the effort. The
> discovery of reality will continue only if we
> abandon outworn formulas...What is the use...
> if it only concludes in a new formalism soon
> as sclerotic as the old one was?...Nothing
> in art is ever won for good...But the
> movement of these evolutions and revolutions
> constitutes its perpetual renaissance.[74]

Thus, it is a mistake to impose on reality that form
of anthropomorphism which was so admired in older writer
like Balzac, who established the mood or tone of a story
by anthropomorphized descriptions of inanimate objects,
such as the furniture in a room. Traditional critics

> make it the sole... criterion of all praise as of
> all reproach, to identify...a precise reflection
> on man, his situation in the world...with a
> certain anthropocentric atmosphere, vague but
> imbuing all things, giving the world its so-
> called significance, investing it from within by
> a more or less disingenious network of sentiments
> and thoughts.[75]

The new critic, on the other hand, will reject all human
projection, or anthropomorphism.

> He sees [things], but he refuses to appropriate
> them, he refuses to maintain any suspect under-
> standing with them, any complicity; he asks
> nothing of them...[76]

> The world around us turns back into a smooth
> surface, without significance, without soul,
> without values...we find ourselves once again
> facing things.[77]

Instead of this universe of "signification"

94

(psychological, social, functional), we must
try then, to construct a world both more solid
and more immediate. Let it be first of all
by their presence that objects and gestures
establish themselves.[78]

Although this sounds remarkably like the program of
Sartre and Camus to honestly face reality stripped of
all human projection, all human illusions, Robbe-Grillet
criticizes Sartre and Camus for continuing that romantic
projection of human concerns onto the world, the "pathetic
fallacy" of traditional fictional narrative. And, of
course, Robbe-Grillet is correct. As we have seen, the
tragedy of absurdity can only arise from the privative
comparison of reality with man's hopes and desires.
Only with the expectation of what we want of reality does
reality's indifference to that expectation strike us
tragically as a rejection, or refusal. It is this
lingering romantic humanism in absurdist writing which
Robbe-Grillet attacks. In The Stranger, for example, he
says,

> existence in it is characterized by the presence
> of interior distances, and...nausea is man's
> unhappy visceral penchant for these distances...
> Is this really to take the "side" of things, to
> represent them from "their own point of view"? [79]

For Robbe-Grillet absurdity is still too humanly attached.
It presupposes a suspect metaphysical synthesis of
essence and existence. We must overcome the tendency
toward this metaphysical romanticism, transcending the
absurd longing for meaning toward a genuinely neutral
confrontation with reality, which is neither rational nor
irrational, but simply a-rational.

> Is it a question of what is called the absurd?
> Certainly not...It is, that's all. But there
> is a risk for the writer: with the suspicion
> of absurdity the metaphysical danger returns.
> Non-sense, a-causality, and the void irresist-
> ibly attract higher worlds and super natures...[80]

But can we escape all human subjectivity and projection
in our approach to reality? I am convinced we cannot,
but the reader can judge for himself whether or not Robbe-
Grillet succeeds in the following passages, or whether,
like Sartre and Camus, he simply projects his own
attitude of human indifference. In Le Voyeur, for
example, he seems to continue the kind of neutral,
geometrical description Sartre begins in Nausea of the

ink-bottle box ("...it's a parallelopiped rectangle, it opens--"), though in this case it is a description of a waterfront pier.

> The stone rim -- an oblique, sharp edge formed
> by two intersecting perpendicular planes: the
> vertical embankment perpendicular to the quay
> and the ramp leading to the top of the pier --
> was continued along its upper side at the top
> of the pier by a horizontal line extending
> straight toward the quay.

Does this describe the "naked World" or does it express Robbe-Grillet's cold, hard-edged, purely visual attitude toward things? Or, let the reader judge for himself the neutral objectivity of this more general statement of a "stubborn, defiant" realty.

> But the world is neither significant nor
> absurd. It is, quite simply...And suddenly
> the obviousness of this strikes us with
> irrestible force. All at once the whole
> splendid construction collapses; opening
> our eyes unexpectedly, we have experienced
> ...the shock of this stubborn reality we
> were pretending to have mastered. Around
> us, defying the noisy pack of our animistic
> or protective adjectives, things are there.[81]

Chapter Three: References

1. Mary Warnock, _Existentialism_ (London: Oxford University Press, 1970), p. 1.

2. John Wild, _The New Empiricism_ (Englewood Cliffs: Prentice-Hall, 1962), p. 427.

3. Jean-Paul Sartre, _Being and Nothingness_, Hazel Barnes, trans. (New York: Philosophical Library, 1956). p. xlv.

4. _Ibid._, p. xlvii.

5. _Ibid._, p. xlix.

6. Klaus Hartman, _Sartre's Ontology_ (Evanston: Northwestern University Press, 1966), p. 33.

7. Warnock, _op. cit._, p. 196.

8. Sartre, _op. cit._, p. lxi.

9. _Ibid._, pp. lxiii-lxvi.

10. _Ibid._, p. 7.

11. _Ibid._, p. 76.

12. Martin Heidegger, _Being and Time_, John McQuarrie and Edward Robinson, trans. (London: S.C.M. Press, 1962), p. 78.

13. _Ibid._, p. 95.

14. _Ibid._, p. 97.

15. _Ibid._.

16. _Ibid._, p. 188-192.

17. Sartre, _op. cit._, p. 18.

18. _Ibid._, p. 24.

19. _Ibid._, p. 44.

20. _Ibid._, pp. 173-175.

21. Ibid., p. 181.

22. Ibid., p. 179.

23. Ibid., p. 177.

24. Ibid., p. 81.

25. Ibid., pp. 82-83.

26. Ibid., p. 202.

27. Ibid., p. 83.

28. Ibid., p. 181.

29. Ibid., p. 197.

30. Ibid., p. 218.

31. Ibid., p. 619.

32. Ibid., p. 617.

33. Ibid., pp. 171-172.

34. Ibid., p. 624.

35. Wild, op. cit., p. 143.

36. Hartmann, op. cit., p. 40.

37. Ibid., p. 39.

38. Ibid., p. 135.

39. Jean-Paul Sartre, Nausea, Lloyd Alexander, tran
(New York: New Directions, 1964), p. 1.

40. Ibid.

41. Ibid., pp. 19-20.

42. Ibid., p. 2.

43. Ibid., p. 3.

44. Jean-Paul Sartre, "Existentialism and Humanism
Philip Mairet, trans., in Morton White, ed., The Age of
Analysis (New York: Mentor Books, 1955), p. 122.

45. Ibid., p. 123.

46. Sartre, Nausea, op. cit., p. 10.

47. Ibid., p. 122.

48. Ibid., p. 98.

49. Ibid., p. 125.

50. Ibid., pp. 126-127.

51. Ibid., p. 169.

52. Ibid., p. 130.

53. Ibid., pp. 130-131.

54. Henri Bergson, An Introduction to Metaphysics, T.E. Hulme, trans. (New York: The Liberal Arts Press, 1949), p. 50.

55. Sartre, Nausea, op. cit., p. 131.

56. Ibid., p. 159.

57. Ibid., p. 128.

58. Ibid., p. 134.

59. Ibid., p. 13.

60. Ibid., p. 95-96.

61. Ibid., p. 96.

62. Ibid., p. 56.

63. Ibid., pp. 132-133.

64. Ibid., p. 128.

65. Ibid., p. 135.

66. Ibid., p. 111.

67. Ibid., p. 126.

68. Ibid., p. 127.

69. Ibid., pp. 76-77.

70. *Ibid.*, p. 133.

71. *Ibid.*, p. 129.

72. *Ibid.*, p. 175.

73. *Ibid.*, p. 178.

74. Alain Robbe-Grillet, "From Realism to Reality," in *For A New Novel*, Richard Howard, trans. (New York: Grove Press, 1965), pp. 158-159.

75. Robbe-Grillet, "Nature, Humanism, Tragedy," *ibid.*, pp. 51-52.

76. *Ibid.*, p. 52

77. *Ibid.*, p. 71.

78. Robbe-Grillett, "A Future for the Novel," *ibid.*, p. 21.

79. Robbe-Grillet, "Nature, Humanism, Tragedy," *op. cit.*, p. 68.

80. Robbe-Grillet, "From Realism to Reality," *op. cit* pp. 163-164.

81. Robbe-Grillet, "A Future for the Novel," *op. cit.* p. 19.

CHAPTER 4: IONESCO

Ionesco develops many of the themes of absurdity
discussed in previous chapters, but with a greater
balance between the heavy and light phases of absurdity
and with a decided movement, in the evolution of his
work, from the oppressive heaviness of absurdity toward
its euphoric lightness, a movement we will see carried
still further in Beckett. Most of his work appears
to revolve around these predominantly metaphysical themes,
as Ionesco himself has frequently pointed out.

> Two fundamental states of consciousness are
> at the root of all my plays. Sometimes one
> dominates, sometimes the other; sometimes they
> are mingled. These two basic feelings are
> those of evanescence on the one hand, and of
> heaviness on the other;...of light and of
> heavy shadows....All of us have felt at times
> that the world is made of some dreary substance,
> that walls no longer have any thickness. We
> seem to see through everything in a universe
> without space, made up only of light and color;
> all our existence, all the history of the
> world becomes at this moment useless, senseless,
> impossible. When one does not succeed in going
> beyond this first step of disorientation...,
> the sensation of evanescence results in a
> feeling of anguish, a sort of dizziness....
> But all this can just as well become euphoric:
> Anguish is suddenly transformed into liberty;
> nothing is important any longer but the wonder
> of being....This state of consciousness is
> very rare....I am most often under the dominance
> of the opposite feeling: Lightness changes to
> heaviness...; the world weighs heavily; the
> universe crushes me. A curtain, an insuper-
> able wall comes between me and the world...;
> matter fills everything, takes up all space;
> annihilates all liberty under its weight;
> the horizon shrinks and the world becomes a
> stifling dungeon...[1]

Practically all of Ionesco's work relates directly
or indirectly to a recurring experience which he had
as an adolescent and which he refers to frequently
as the most crucial of his life.

101

I felt everything was emptying away...it was
like a release, things lost their weight
around me, I was cutting adrift from things and
they were losing all arbitrary, conventional
significance, all that enormous mass of meanings
of all sorts...amidst which I had been trapped,
that labyrinth of tangled paths in which I
had lost my way. Everything was now per-
vaded by a dazzling light, and...I became
aware, with limitless joy, that everything
exists...in a heavenly light, delicate,
fragile....Yet in one instant things became
once again heavy, opaque and dark....I myself
seemed to grow heavy again, dense, heavy as
lead, a mere thing that emptiness can eat
away.[2]

Unlike Sartre and Camus, Ionesco has developed a
style of writing which more perfectly matches the absurdist content. Instead of asserting that consciousness
has become detached from reality, Ionesco demonstrates
this in a use of language which is itself detached and
disjointed. Rather than describe the psychological
moods of oppressive heaviness and evanescent lightness,
Ionesco buries his characters beneath masses of furniture or has them walking on air. Rather than argue,
as Roquentin does in Nausea, that things can become
anything, eggs actually metamorphize in Ionesco's
plays into people, who then become slabs of meat, etc.
The form of expression, in other words, has become inseparable from its content. As Camus put it, the philosophical ideas have been thoroughly integrated into
concrete images. Ionesco himself puts it this way.

The philosopher thinks by philosphizing, the
painter thinks by painting....A playwright is
a man who thinks by writing his dramas or
comedies....the dialogue and movement of the
stage are the author's particular way of
exploring reality...the language of literature...is by no means an illustration or
vulgarization of some other, superior language
....It's often the artist's language which
stimulates and organizes the thought of
others, which creates new ways of seeing the
world.[3]

This new form gives Ionesco's work a power and direct-
ness lacking in even the best fiction of Sartre and
Camus. Ionesco makes the point himself in an almost

102

brutal way, though modestly omitting his own name from those with whom he contrasts Sartre and Camus.

> [Sartre and Camus] were talking about absurdity and death, but...they never really lived these themes, ...they did not feel them within themselves in an almost irrational, visceral way... All this was not deeply inscribed in their language...With Adamov and Beckett it really is a very naked reality that is conveyed through the apparent dislocation of language.[4]

Unfortunately, however, this very synthesis of form and content makes it exceedingly difficult to "translate" or even understand his plays. As a result the metaphysical thrust of his work is often misunderstood as a sociological concern with the failure of human communication in modern society, despite Ionesco's repeated protestations to the contrary.

In this first part of this chapter we will work through this misunderstanding as a convenient way of exploring Ionesco's conception of the absurd. Language, of course, is an important theme in all of Ionesco's work, and the dislocation of language is certainly the single most striking feature of his unusual style. In addition, it is this aspect of his work which dominates his earliest period (the first three plays, especially The Bald Soprano) which established Ionesco as a writer of the first rank. Add to this the fact that the communication theme was introduced to the English-speaking public by no less a critic than Kenneth Tynan, and we can begin to appreciate the tenacity of this persistent interpretation. In the 1950's Ionseco was introduced to many who had never read or seen his plays as a nihilist obsessed with the breakdown of society following the second World War. Ionesco himself offers a very different interpretation of his own work.

Like all great art, Ionesco's plays operate on many different, interpenetrating levels at once--social, psychological, historical, religious and philosophical. Thus, for example, the image of heaviness can legitimately be understood in some of his plays as social conformity (Victims of Duty, A Stroll in the Air, Jack and The Lesson), and in others, as human brutality (The Killer, Amédée, The Lesson and Victims of Duty), and in some of these plays, as both. Nonetheless, it is the metaphysical dimension which forms the underlying structure of the plays in the light of which the other, subordinant themes must be understood.

103

It is not ordinary human communication which has broken down, but only, as in Nausea, the ultimate metaphysical failure of words to communicate reality absolutely, as it is in itself. It is not a historical change which has suddenly affected the ability of people to communicate verbally which concerns Ionesco, but a profound reflection on the absolute limits of any language to describe reality completely, as it is in itself.

In The Observer 1958 Tynan ("Ionesco, Man of Destiny?")said that Ionesco's plays, in particular The Bald Soprano, represented a rejection of reality where all communication was impossible and words were completely meaningless. In Conversations with Eugene Ionesco (not translated into English until 1971) Ionesco roundly refutes this interpretation of his work. We are not socially isolated, but do quite easily communicate with one another.

> About the crisis of language today: actually
> no such crisis exists....There's no such thing
> as the impossibility of communication, except
> as a single case: between me and myself.
> Socially, everything is communicable...words
> are there, clear and precise, to say what
> there is to be said. We deliberately conceal
> our thoughts, while revealing them....What
> there is to be said can be said. What needs
> to be said, that which is existence and not
> just a thing, this alone refuses to be said.[5]

As in Nausea it is only that extraordinary reflection on the relation of thought and language to reality which necessarily, evades linguistic description. Ordinary communication is not only possible but easily accessible In The Bald Soprano, Ionesco says,

> I wasn't concerned with the impossibility of
> communication or with solitude. Quite the
> contrary. I am in favor of solitude....
> It's easy to communicate. Man is never
> really alone; and if he's unhappy, it's
> because he's never really alone.[6]

What Ionesco is expressing in this play and others is the totally transparent absorption of most people in their blindly projected linguistic and conceptual formulae on the world, a projection which makes the world familiar, commonplace and mundane, an absorption

in the world which makes ordinary communication possible
but which also makes us blind to what Sartre called
"existence." In Ionesco's work he contrasts the naive
state of ordinary consciousness with the sheer wonder
and novelty of the world when we become conscious of
that projection, distancing ourselves from it so that
forms of communication cease to be naively accepted and
become, for the first time, strange and opaque. From
that point of view it seems amazing that people can
live and communicate so easily and nonchalantly within
such a conventional world.

> There is a degree of communication between
> people....They understand one another. That's
> what's so astounding....If, intentionally, you
> put yourself completely outside everything, on
> one floor above what's going on, if you look
> at people as though they were part of a show
> and you yourself were a being from another
> world looking down on what's happening here,
> then you wouldn't understand anything, words
> would be hollow, everything would be empty.
> You can get this feeling if you block your
> ears when you're watching people dancing....
> Their movements are senseless. I write
> plays to express this feeling of astonish-
> ment.[7]

Clearly, the failure of communication is not to be
understood on an ordinary mundane level, but as a
theatrical device for exposing that mundane outlook in
which words naively attach to objects, and to reveal in
its place that wonderful and terrifying "naked Reality"
which appears once the ordinary, comfortable acceptance
of linguistic conventions has been stripped away.

> Once people have accepted existence; once
> they've moved inside it, everything stops
> being amazing or absurd. Once they've accepted
> the idea of being on the inside they start to
> communicate. When you step outside, move
> away and take a good look, you stop communi-
> cating.[8]

As with Roquentin in Nausea, on the ordinary mundane
level there is no problem naming and describing a streetcar seat, a tree root or a glass of beer. This is done
as a matter of course precisely because the relationship of words to object is never called into question,
but is naively taken for granted, words simply attaching
to objects. Once that relation is called into question

105

both the word and the object take on a new look quite independently of its association with the other. As we noted in the first chapter, a meaningful world is the product of the synthesis of essence and existence, while their seapration is the cause of absurdity and meaninglessness. Only in that extraordinary experience of their separation do objects appear strange and words lose their meanings.

> I wanted this play [The Bald Soprano] to ex-
> press the feeling of strangeness that the
> world inspires in me. The characters are
> completely emptied of their content; so are
> their words. For instance, you may say, or
> hear, the word "horse." You can understand
> the phrase, "I am getting on my horse."
> But it's possible for the word to get emp-
> tied of its content, for you no longer to
> hear anything but the sound, "horse, horse,
> horse." Sometimes it's not only the sound,
> it's all reality that's emptied of its con-
> tent.[9]

Thus, far from deploring the failure of ordinary communication, Ionesco is trying to create it! He attempts
to jar us out of a familiar world where ordinary communication is possible into a strange, new world in
which language stands at a distance from reality.

At the same time, however, absorption in a commonly
accepted world which makes ordinary communication possible thwarts the revelation and communication of
genuinely personal insights into the world. Thus the
conditions which make ordinary communication possible
are precisely those which prevent the more profound
disclosure between individuals--that truly personal
communication which Sartre argues is simply impossible.
Carried to an extreme, complete acceptance of and
absorption in the linguistic conventions which make
projection possible reduces all language to the level
of the cliché and robs language of any personal
discovery or individual interpretation. To focus
sharply on the transparency of unthinking, naive pro-
ection of conventional, mass meaning, Ionesco has reduce
the characters in The Bald Soprano to this impersonal
level of cliché.

> They don't want to communicate, they have no
> desire to....They don't think....They inhabit
> the world of the impersonal, the world of the

collective....In short, the characters in
my plays are people who pronounce slogans to
save themselves the trouble of thinking.[10]

In the language of Nausea, they don't "exist." By
reducing his characters to total transparency, Ionesco
shocks his audience into a virtual state of complete
opacity in which we see, perhaps for the first time, the
conventionality of our own language, our thought, our
feelings--even our most "private" feelings, and we see
clearly that words are not attached to objects but
exist altogether independently. On a more superficial
level the distancing affected by Ionesco's plays might
make us see only the arbitrary constructions of obviously
conformist clichés, making us feel superior to people
who engage in this form of trite conversation, but on
a deeper level we see that this effects all forms of
thought and speech, from the most banal to the most
profound. All are human constructions, reality transcends them all.

Even the theory of absurdity, oddly enough.   This
is not "the one truth" which shows all other theories
to be shallow or false, but is itself simply one more
humanly constructed interpretation of the world from a
particular human standpoint. All views of the world are
absurd in this sense, even the absurdist view, as
Ionesco is well aware. "It is absurd to say that the
world is absurd."[11] As Camus also was aware, to call
the world absurd presupposes some absolute stance from
which to make this judgment, a stance explicitly denied
by the absurdist point of view.

If I denounce the absurd, I transcend the
absurd by the very fact of my denunciation.
For by what right should I declare a thing to
be absurd, unless I had before me the image...
of something that was not absurd.[12]

But this is the very transcendence which the absurdist
position denies. "We cannot soar above it all, we
cannot be superior to the Divinity....That's a piece of
folly."[13]

Thus, Ionesco's view of communication is considerably richer and more complex than is generally recognized. Although ordinary communication takes place
within, and even requires, that naive absorption in
social stereotypes in which linguistic forms are simply
transparent, ideal communication, Ionesco believes,

exists only within a tension between conventional forms
of expression and individual perception. In order to
reveal some new aspect of reality, a form of speech must
break with the stereotype and explore the world from a
fresh, individual perspective. But this new form of
expression will remain unintelligible and opaque
until it is translated into more conventional symbols
or until the new form of communication becomes commonly
accepted. But in either case, the freshness of the
original insight tends to get lost in a new stereotype.
In order to break through this stereotype to a new
vision of reality, new forms of expression must be
sought, and so the cycle begins again. It is within
this tension of old and new, originality and cliché,
transparent and opaque that Ionesco holds important
communication takes place.

A form of expression which is traditional is
scarcely noticed as a form of speech but becomes a
transparent window through which the object appears.
But a form of expression which is new and not yet
accepted, like Ionesco's own plays, attracts attention
to itself, becoming therefore opaque and difficult to
understand. With understanding and acceptance of the
new conventions comes communication, but this eventually
leads to the cliché.

> Things are incommunicable in the beginning
> because they have not yet been communicated,
> and incommunicable in the end because the
> expressions that prop them up have been worn
> out.[14]

> When a thing or an idea is fashionable, it's
> often mere repetition--a cliché emptied of
> its content, its truth, its discovery. On
> the other hand, obviously every work is rooted
> in time...the time it's written in...which is
> why all worthwhile literary works stand at the
> crossroads between time and eternity.[15]

It is not the form of speech itself which is either
meaningful or meaningless, but the way in which it is
received by human speakers. The very same form of
words can be at one time a breathtaking revelation and
at another time a banal cliché. Meaningful forms of
thought and language must therefore be constantly re-
freshing, revitalizing themselves, since, however significant, they eventually gravitate toward the accepted,
the familiar and the trite. In Present Past, Past Present
Ionesco speaks of the evolution of all forms of speech

from revelation to cliché as the product of the inevitable transparency which occurs when forms of thought and
speech become conventionalized.

> [We are] lost in the impersonal world of the
> "one"; it is necessary, therefore, to put
> everything in question again, it is necessary
> to reconsider the very basis of speech, to
> go back to axioms... But each new system of
> expression, once it has become a convention,
> or an acquisition, or a cliché, or an ideo-
> logy, loses its essential truth. Life be-
> comes a word.[16]

For Ionesco the primary purpose of art is to guide
this necessary reviving of language, in which words no
longer revolve around themselves, but become instruments
for new ways of seeing the world.

> Every work of art is the materialization of
> an almost indescribable personal experience,
> it is putting a language in question again,
> it is a rediscovery or a discovery of the
> world seen by the poet for the first time.
> The poet cannot invent new words...of course.
> But the handling of the words...renews them.
> The reader...must in turn be able to receive
> this new virginity.[17]

Of course, as Ionesco realizes, the same degenerating
process must affect his own work, and indeed is already
occuring.

> Alas, all the sincerity, all the authenticity,
> all the truth, everything that I have lived and
> felt all by myself is already disappearing in
> clichés, expressions that belong to the public
> patrimony and to men in general.[18]

Elsewhere Ionesco remarks on the way in which the
radical dislocating techniques of absurdist writing is
fast becoming an accepted convention.

> What once looked like the dislocation of
> language now seems very clear to us. The
> way of expressing a certain disaster is
> starting to congeal again and increasing the
> distance between us and the disaster. This
> disjointed language has reconstructed itself
> in another way; or rather, the dislocation,
> having as it were congealed, now looks to us

like a new coherence...perhaps I should say,
like a new crust, an armour. This is why the
great themes have always to be reworked,
relived, re-examined.[19]

As Robbe-Grillet also points out, even the attempt
to reject the "profound transcendent" in favor of the
"immediate significance" of things

risks...transcendence (metaphysics loves a
vacuum, and rushes into it like smoke up a
chimney); for, within immediate significance,
we find the absurd, which is theoretically
nonsignificance, but which as a matter of
fact leads immediately to a new transcendence;
and the infinite fragmentation of immediate
meaning thus establishes a new totality,
quite as dangerous, quite as futile.[20]

Language can communicate, then, but it need not;
and meaningful discourse is certainly not automatic.
Thus Ionesco frequently distinguishes ordinary polite
talk from meaningful discourse.

One can speak without thinking; for this we
have clichés....The only true thought is living
thought.[21]

Sometimes he marks the distinction as that between
"language in general" and the "spoken word" of the
individual.

There is language in general, on the one
hand, and the spoken speech of the individual,
on the other. I am not in language in general.
I am in the spoken word.[22]

And, like Camus, he often contrasts the inadequacy of
words with the power of images.

It's as though by writing books I had worn out
all symbols without getting to the heart of
them. They no longer speak to me with living
voices. Words have killed images or concealed
them....Words are not speech.[23]

Images are so concise, so profound and complex,
and words are so inadequate to translate living
thought.[24]

Words "hide" or "mask" reality because, through the adoption of linguistic conventions, we confuse word and object, the word then replaces the object and words begin to stand between us and the world they are meant to reveal. The situation is not hopeless, however, since words can reveal aspects of reality if they are understood as what they are, namely conventions for focusing on a particular aspect of the world as seen from a particular human point of view.

What is needed, then, is a new understanding of the relationship of thought and language to reality, which Ionesco suggests in several of his prose works. First we must realize that we cannot grasp reality as it is in itself, that reality and our understanding of it are always and necessarily distinct.

> The world in itself is not knowable. Because
> there is only consciousness of the world, which
> means that for Husserl, as for Kant, reality
> in itself cannot be grasped...; it exists but
> it does not exist for me.[25]

Like the other absurdists, Ionesco is thus a realist and a dualist. There is a reality independent of us and there are human forms of thought and speech which highlight facets of that reality from predetermined human points of view. But word and object, thought and reality are never identical and never completely coincide; each transcends the other.

> The philosopher thinks by philosophizing. The
> painter thinks by painting; painting is the
> form of his thought, it is his thought....
> This simply proves that reality, or the world,
> appears under a multiplicity of aspects to
> the many and various temperaments of men....
> In my view, a playwright is a man who thinks
> by writing his dramas or comedies....
> Knowledge...is also construction...since
> any knowledge, any encounter between self and
> the world is a projection of the self into...
> the world, a projection, that's to say a
> pattern, a shape, an architecture....A whole
> world is built up, or disclosed, as the artist
> writes it and thinks it.[26]

Our view of the world, then, is a human creation, but if, in our blind acceptance of that view, we forget its human invention, we confuse word and object and get locked into the staid, linguistically demarcated world from which Ionesco's plays seek to release us.

It is important to realize that for Ionesco, unlike
Sartre and Camus, this release can be a joyous, euphoric
experience, acting as a counterbalance to the leaden
heaviness of absurdity we found in Sartre. Once we
realize the creativity of human thought and its distinction from reality, we see things as divorced from
their names and hence as alien and heavy, but, for
Ionesco at any rate, we can also experience this as a
release from a static, regimented, collectivized world
into a fresh vision of reality as absolutely transcending
all linguistic boundaries, demarcations, limits and
therefore as limitless and in that sense, empty or
transparent. The parallels to mystic exaltation are
unmistakable and will be discussed later. In one of
his autobiographical recollections of that crucial
boyhood experience to which much of his later work relate
he writes,

> Once, long ago, I was sometimes overcome by a
> sort of grace, a euphoria. It was as if...
> every notion, every reality was emptied of
> its content. After this emptiness, after
> this dizzy spell, it was as if I found myself
> suddenly at the center of pure, ineffable
> existence; it was as if things had freed
> themselves of all arbitrary labels...It did
> not seem to me that I was the victim of a
> nominalist crisis; on the contrary, I think
> that I became one with the one essential
> reality, when, along with an immense, serene
> joy, I was overcome by what I might call the
> ...certainty of being, the certainty that the
> social order, politics, language, organized
> thought, systems and systematizations...
> were pure nothingness...[27]

In this last sentence, we get a clear idea of the forces
of social conformity opposing the vision of euphoric
lightness which occupy a central place in many of his
plays.

As a result of this vision, he goes on to say, word
and object become detached, each standing out from the
other, revealing both as strange and new. Sometimes this
dislocation of word and object was brought about in the
kind of game children often play, repeating a word over
and over again until it sounds "funny," that is, until

the word-sound separates itself off from its customary
meaning.

> Often this began in an unexpected way, when I
> would pronounce the most ordinary word; paper
> for example. It was as if the word disappeared,
> a word that had replaced a reality that it had
> imprisoned and hidden...I became totally con-
> scious that meanings, that words are arbitrary,
> mere labels...[28]

As human meaning recedes from reality the systematic
architecture it imposes on reality also retreats, resulting in a kind of emptiness, not empty like a new house,
but, as toward the end of <u>Nausea</u>, empty of all human
demarcations separating objects, marking them off from
one another.

> Walls collapsed, definitions were dislocated...
> The names of things drew apart from things...
> Our reality broke up into thousands of pieces,
> went up in smoke, then the smoke blew away, and
> there was nothing now but this immense sun...
> Everything that I had thought to be solidly
> built was only castles of cards that had
> tumbled down.[29]

> It began with the feeling that space was
> emptying itself of its material heaviness
> ...Notions were freed of their content.
> Objects became transparent, permeable; they
> were no longer obstacles and it seemed as
> if one could pass through them...I felt as
> if I had received a blow right in the heart
> ...dissolving the limits of things, breaking
> down definitions, abolishing the meaning of
> things...as the light seemed to make the walls
> and the house I was walking by disappear.[30]

But the exhilarating experience of lightness is immediately
overcome by its opposite pole of heaviness.

> It lasted a few second...[then] the miraculous
> evidence vanished. The sky became just a sky
> ...Things, the walls, took on their usual form
> again...All that was left was this world of...
> shadows,...the everyday world took its usual
> place again.[31]

A major theme in Ionesco's latest plays is how to achieve

and retain this experience of lightness.

Returning to the point from which we started, we do have more or less adequate means of communicating with o another, exploring, describing, enumerating the things i our world. But it is this very facility which hides us from the fact that the world transcends all these system of explanation. Ionesco's work is designed to bring abo that unusual experience in which we see the humanly base conventionality of all our thoughts and interpretations and see the world as transcending altogether human modes of expression.

There are times when the world seems emptied of
all expression, all content. There are times when
we look at it as though we'd just that moment
been born, and then it looks astonishing and
inexplicable. Of course, we have plenty of
explanations to hand! ...Only these systems
fade the moment we have this primordial feeling...[3]

The concept of the original freshness of our percep tion of the world is, of course, a Romantic view. As children everything is new and wonderful; then, as Wordsworth pointed out, as we grow older we take things for granted and the wonderful freshness of the world is lost in a dull familiarity. "The end of childhood is when things cease to astonish us. When the world seems familiar..one has become adult."[33] Yet as adults we recover an odd sort of second childhood, in which we pretend that the world is really just as comfortable and familiar as our projected systems of thought and languag have made it out to be.

Then, I believe most human beings forget what
they have understood, recover another sort of
childhood that, for some of them, for a very
few, can last all their lives. It is not a
true childhood, but a kind of forgetting.[34]

In this essentially Romantic terminology, the purpo of Ionseco's plays is quite simply to recover that lost insight of the child. As he records in an old diary, after adolescence Ionesco himself experienced the dazzling light vision less and less frequently, though, throughout his adult life, he could occasionally recover it.

I sometimes wake up, become conscious, realize
that I am surrounded by things and by people,
and if I look closely at the sky or the wall or
the earth or the hand writing or not writing, I

have the impression that I'm seeing it all for
the first time, then, as it were, the first time,
I wonder, or I ask, "what's that?"[35]

This is often followed by the experience of evanescent
lightness.

Then...a sudden light, a great blinding light
floods over everything, obliterating all meaning,
all our preoccupations, all those shadows, that's
to say all those walls that make us imagine limits,
distinctions, separations, significances.[36]

The experience of reality is not, then, the experience
of some new Transcendent Absolute beyond this ordinary
world, but simply the plain, ordinary world stripped of its
conventional conceptual and linguistic formulae.

Nothing seems more surprising to me than that
which is banal; the surreal is there, within
grasp of our hands, in everyday conversation.[37]

But because we normally identify reality with <u>conceptually
interpreted</u> reality, this new experience can equally be
described as unreal or a-real.

A second possible attitude: to consider
reality as something beyond reality, to
be aware of it not as surrealistic but as
unfamiliar, miraculous, a-real. Reality
of the unreal, unreality of the real.[38]

The constant theme in all of Ionesco's plays, then,
is metaphysical absurdity, the separation of language
from reality and a vision of the reality stripped of its
familiar linguistic garb.

So what strikes me as absurd, utterly extraordinary,
is existence itself...The moment there's a gap
between ideology and reality, there's absurdity...
In fact language does nothing but contradict at
every moment an extremely simple and visible
reality, as if everyone were refusing to see
this reality.[39]

It is not the falsity of linguistic description which
contradicts reality, but its transparency. By examining
the transparent familiarity of ordinary conventionalized
thought and language from the standpoint of absurdity,
the ordinary acceptance of the world stands out visibly
opaque and extraordinary. What is unique to Ionesco's

vision of absurdity is its positive, euphoric, light side
as a counter-balance and solution to the Sartrean heaving
of nausea. To gain a more thorough grasp of this aspect
of Ionesco's thought we must turn to the plays themselves

There is a steady progression in the evolution of
Ionesco's plays from the heavy to the light side of absurd
ity. The first group of plays, from 1948 to 1951, deals
largely with the problems of language communication which
we have been discussing. The second group, form 1951 to
1953, are mostly concerned with the mechanical proliferation of heavy, oppressive matter. In the third group,
1953 to 1957, we begin to see a greater emphasis on the
mystical quality of emptiness or lightness which Ionesco
refers to so often in his autobiographical notes, as well
as the transition of heavy to light and back again to
heavy. And, finally, in his latest period, 1963 to 1974
the dominant theme is sheer lightness alone.

Ionesco's first play, The Bald Soprano, was first
performed in 1948. In the play the Martins pay a social
call on the Smiths. They discuss the most trivial banal
ties until firmen arrive to put out an imaginary fire.
There is also the Smith's maid, Mary, who appears from
time to time, somewhat like the chorus of Greek tragedy
or the jester in Elizabethean drama, to make telling
comments on the absurd behavior of the two couples. Three
major themes can be detected in this play, all of which
have to do with the limitations of human discourse. The
first, and most obvious, is the degeneration of language
into clichés. The Smiths announce in deadly earnest to
one another that they are man and wife, live in this
house, have two children, and so on. Ionesco says he got
this idea for the play from studying an introductory
phrase book in English as a foreign language, where such
dialogue takes place. In one stage version (which Ionesco
liked so well he later had it incorporated into the play)
the end of the play returns to the beginning scene of the
Smith's conversation, suggesting that this dreary nonsense
goes on and on ad nauseum. By distancing ourselves from
this exaggerated version of ordinary polite conversation
("How are you?" "Fine, and you?" "Not bad." "How's the
family?" etc.), the play presents a hilarious spoof of
insincere, unthinking, generalized collective talk which
communicates absolutely nothing about the individuals
themselves.

But a more important theme which many reviewers,
including Tynan, failed to detect at first, is the more
subtle metaphysical notion of how truly amazing ordinary
things actually are. The play is not simply a condemnati
of people who pretend that the commonplaces of their lives

have monumental importance--though that element is certainly
present; it is also an attempt to show that from an aloof,
distanced perspective these commonplaces are truly astonishing. What is amazing is that people generally take them
for granted. As Ionesco said of the play some years later,
"Nothing seems more surprising to me than that which is
banal." The play is not perhaps so successful in conveying
this second theme, however.

The third theme is the inability of logical, rational
thought to completely reveal reality as it is in itself.
In the play Mr. and Mrs. Martin construct an elaborate
and ingenious logical proof that they are married to one
another. They establish that each is married and has a
daughter, and that since this daughter has one red and one
white eye, it must be the same daughter and that they are
therefore the parents of this daughter, and so man and
wife. In itself the dialogue is a powerful comment on
people whose consciousness of the world has been totally
absorbed in generalized patterns of thought, speech and
action. They lack that personal intuition which would
make any such argument completely unnecessary. But after
their discovery, Mary enters and, as an aside to the
audience, points out that through one tiny flaw in the
Martin's argument, the conclusion is falsified, and they
are not in fact married to one another after all.

> Mary: I can let you in on a secret. Elizabeth
> is not Elizabeth, Donald is not Donald. And
> here is the proof: the child that Donald spoke
> of is not Elizabeth's daughter...Whereas Donald's
> daughter has a white right eye and a red left
> eye, Elizabeth's child has a red right eye and
> a white left eye! Thus all of Donald's system
> of deduction collapses when it comes up against
> this last obstacle which destroys his whole
> theory...But who is the true Donald? Who is the
> true Elizabeth? Who has any interest in prolong-
> ing this confusion? I don't know. Let's not
> try to know. Let's leave things as they are.

There is a similarly indecisive conclusion to the
debate later in the play as to whether the fireman rang
the door-bell. The most obvious point of this, of course,
is the fallibility of rational systems of proof and
argumentation. The conclusion rests on the truth of all
the premises; if only one of these proves false, the whole
theory collapses. This coincides with Ionesco's stated
intention of exposing the inadequzcy of our verbalized
understanding of reality by picking apart its weaknesses
one by one. Nonetheless I think the important point is

a more subtle one. What is amazing about the proof is that is goes as far as it does toward establishing Donald's and Elizabeth's matrimony, though not quite all the way. As Camus said, we are able to understand a great deal about the world, and explain and prove a great many things within it, but we can never get to the absolute bottom of things, and this shifts our attention, not to the foolishness of logical or scientific explanation, but to the broader metaphysical theme of the absolute distinction of word and object, thought and reality. This is what has become known as the "mystery" element in absurdist fiction. A problem is posed, its solution seems immanent but at the last moment breaks down, and we are left with an unexplained problem. The point, again, is not that things are totally unexplainable or meaningless, but that they are not completely or absolutely explainable. The fallacy in Donald's argument, after all, is established by Mary's equally logical proof. The mystery element is a successful literary device for suggesting a notion of reality just beyond our grasp, like the carrot Sartre refers to just beyond the reach of the donkey. This is one solution to the dilemma how to describe the thing in itself which by definition cannot be described--the absurdist writer simply shows <u>that</u> forms of thought never completely capture or exhaust the object, that the object therefore always transcends our attempts to explain it. It is not that explanations are false or inaccurate, but that they are not identical with the things they do explain. Explanations are useful human devices for relating bits of experience into a humanly intelligible order, but they are human projections; they are not identical with the very fabric of reality.

In the other two plays of the first period, <u>The Lesson</u> and <u>Jack</u>, Ionesco develops the idea of the tyranny of language cut off from reality. When words cease to expose an aspect of reality from a personal human point of view, words can take on a menacing life of their own. In his second play, <u>The Lesson</u>, 1950, an eager and attractive young female student visits a professor for a private lesson. At first the professor is shy, retiring and polite; but gradually he assumes command and verbally dominates the girl who is reduced from a pleasantly bright girl to a mumbling imbecile. As the professor grows in strength and the student gradually weakens, she expresses a growing drowsiness and fatigue which is the first of Ionesco's images of absurd heaviness, appearing in this early play as a response to human tyranny through linguistic conformity. Finally, the professor murders the girl,

in one version with the word "knife," in another, thro
a violent sexual attack. The maid, who, as in The Bald
Soprano, appears from time to time, warns the professor
he is going too far, and, as she announces the professor
next student, informs the audience that this is his 50th
victim, which brings down the curtain.

In Jack or the Submission, 1950, the central theme
is the subjugation of the individual to the collective
mentality of the group as expressed in linguistic conventions. At first Jack refuses to accept conventional
values; in particular, he refuses to say "I love fried
potatoes" and to accept a conventional marital relation
with Roberte, his family's choice. His parents and
sister plead with him to be reasonable.

Jack: There's nothing I can do about it, I
was born like this...I've done all that was
in my power!

Mother Robert: What an unfeeling heart....

Father Robert: He's an intransigent stranger....

To emphasize the interchangeable uniformity of group
thinking, many of the characters in this and others of
Ionesco's plays have the same name, viz., Robert or
Roberte.

At first, like Camus' stranger, Jack refuses to
conform to this collective mentality. But then he
reluctantly retracts and agrees to love fried potatoes.
Then an interesting twist occurs which robs Jack, not
only of the negative heroism of Camus' stranger, but of
the rewards of social conformity as well. Jack begins
to articulate his own personal view of things (he
prefers girls with three noses, for example); Roberte
accepts his vision of the world, sprouting the desired
number of noses (the first indication of the proliferation image of the later plays), and they begin to plan
their own individualized life together. Finally Jack
realizes he has been trapped; they are simply constructing new conventions.

Jack: I refused to accept....They assured me
that someone would devise a remedy. They
promised me some decorations...they swore
they would give me satisfaction....I made other
criticisms in order finally to declare to
them that I preferred to withdraw...they
implored me to hope....I fell for it!

118

> But everything was false....Ah, they had
> lied to me...and how to escape? They boarded
> up the doors, the windows with nothing,
> they've taken away the stairs....Anything is
> preferable to my present situation. Even
> a new one. [I.e., with Roberte]

This is an interesting dramatization of Ionesco's
notion discussed earlier of the inevitable degeneration
of individual insight into conventionality. Jack's
unique, individual solution, with which he was lured
into a compromising, partial acceptance, has become the
familiar rut everyone else is in. In this statement of
Jack's we see another early attempt to articulate
dramatically the heaviness of absurdity under the guise
of social conformity blocking the passage to freedom.
Here the central problem of absurd heaviness is suggested
which the later plays develop and then try to solve.
Linguistic conformity, as a symbol for social conformity
generally, ties us to a narrow, stereotypical view of the
world alien to our deepest individual instincts. Our
only world is a world devised by others. In Jack
there seems no escape, no way to withdraw. Later, the
theme of lightness is explored as a solution to Jack's
dilemma.

The image of proliferating matter as a symbol for
the heavy side of absurdity, which appears tangentially
in the earlier plays, is the central focus for Ionesco's
second group of plays. The first of these plays, The
Future is in Eggs, or It Takes All Sorts to Make a World,
1951, continues the story of Jack and Roberte, who
hatches endless eggs which turn into people and then
into sausages, slabs of meat, etc. This is reminiscent
of Roquentin's vision that anything can happen, that
objects could become anything. It is first a way of
breaking down our familiar acceptance of the way things
"naturally" or inevitably are, exposing how remarkable,
unaccountable ordinary things really are from the absurdist point of view. But it is also the image of matter
protruding, blossoming everywhere, filling everything,
choking us, crowding us out, which Sartre refers to as
"nausea."

The Chairs is the first and best of Ionesco's
plays dealing with this theme. In the play an old
couple are preparing for the old man's retirement cere-
mony. He is an insignificant, ordinary lighthouse
keeper who has never received the recognition he feels

119

he deserves. But now everyone, including the Emperor, is coming to the lighthouse to hear his complete and final revelation to the world. He has hired a professional orator to speak for him. During most of the play the old woman brings in more and more chairs for imaginary, nonexistent guests until the room is choked with piled-up furniture. The orator finally does arrive but turns out to be mute, resorting finally to some meaningless gibberish which he writes on a blackboard--which ends the play.

Here again critics tended to fasten on to the most obvious element in the play, the failure of the old couple and their pathetic, delusory attempt to reverse their failure in one final act. But clearly the dominant dramatic element in the play is the proliferation of the chairs. This forms a perfect image of the mutually empty and full, light and heavy aspects of absurdity. The chairs are empty of people and this, like any object of human use momentarily not in use, such as an unoccupied house, simply reinforces their brute materiality, their heaviness. As Ionesco said of the play,

> The subject of the play was nothingness, not failure. It was total absence: chairs without people....It was both multiplication and absence, proliferation and nothingness.[40]

Objects devoid of human meaning, human understanding, especially chairs which are designed for and so cry out for human use, are full of a nonhuman, alien matter, but they are equally empty of any human significance. The chairs are dramatically successful because they represent a concrete instantiation of the existentialist notion of negation discussed in the second chapter. We notice the absence of something just in case we have come to anticiapte its presence. An empty auditorium or playing field is more poignantly empty than a hay field, for example, because it is meant to be occupied by people. In The Chairs this sense of absence is heightened by the invisible guests the old man seats and talks to. As Ionesco wrote to Sylvain Dhomme, the director of the play in its first performance,

> The subject of the play is not the message, nor the failure of life, nor the moral disaster of the two old people, but the chairs themselves; that is to say, the absence of people, the absence of the emperor, the absence of God, the absence of matter, the unreality of the world, metaphysical emptiness. The theme

of the play is nothingness....The invisible
elements must be more and more...real...until
nothingness can be heard, made concrete.[41]

A similar theme is developed in The New Tenant, 1953. A
man moves into an unfurnished apartment; movers begin
bringing in furniture to the room. More and more furniture arrives until the tenant is completely buried
beneath it.

Victims of Duty, 1952, is one of Ionesco's most
successful and complex plays. Choubert, a playwright,
and his wife, Madeleine, answer the door one evening
to a detective in search of a former neighbor neither of
them knows. Instead of leaving immediately, the detective enters, begins asking a few polite questions and,
like the professor in The Lesson, gradually subjects
Choubert to an intense "third degree." There is a
mystery to be solved and the detective is determined to
get to the bottom of it. In a psychoanalytic manner he
demands that Choubert go "deeper" and "deeper" into the
recesses of his mind until he comes up with the solution.
The tone of the play is set by Choubert toward the beginning.

Choubert: All the plays that have ever been
written...have never really been anything but
thrillers....Every play's an investigation
brought to a successful conclusion. There's
a riddle, and it's solved in the final scene.

This is the detective's attitude toward life in general.

Detective: I remain Aristotlelially logical,
true to myself, faithful to my duty....I
don't believe in the absurd, everything hangs
together, everything can be comprehended in
time.

This establishes the dramatic conflict of the play--
whether things can be exhaustively explained or not.
This theme operates on two levels, as a reflection on life
in general and more particularly as a comment on the
realistic theater of rational plot, consistent character, etc. If life is not logical then neither should
the theatre be logical. The form of a play must match
its content. Nicolas, a character in the play who
appears to speak for Ionesco, makes this plain.

Inspiring me with a different logic and a

different psychology. I shall introduce contradiction where there is no contradiction and
where there is no contradiction...we'll get
rid of the principle of identity and unity of
character.

In the play Ionesco does in fact experiment with changing
identities and even interchangeable identities of the
main characters, but only occasionally, not consistently
throughout. From the detective's point of view everything has a solution; if we don't know the answer, we
must find it. But the "deeper" Choubert goes the more
confusing, mysterious the problem becomes.

Like Jack, Choubert feels a social obligation to
cooperate fully with this duly appointed civil servant,
so he submits to the interrogation. But this leads, not
to any solution of the detective's question, which
Choubert knows nothing about, but to a vision of oppressive heaviness--to the heavy side of absurdity. And
this heavy weight drags him down deeper and deeper.

Choubert: I shall be alone in the dark, in the
mud.

This represents the trap of conformity which Jack found
himself in. To absorb oneself in the socially formed
picture of the world is to become immersed in all the
goals, problems, aims implied in that picutre. Thus
our obligation to uphold the social order is rooted in
our acceptance of the world as dictated by the society's
linguistic and cultural conventions. But in Victims of
Duty there appears the first suggestion of a means of
escape. Lower down Choubert begins to feel lighter than
air, evanescent, transparent.

Choubert:...the lightening rends the thick
gloom, and there on the horizon, behind the
storm, a gigantic curtain of darkness is
heavily lifting, gleaming through the shadows,
still as a dream in the midst of the storm, a
magic city,...a bubbling spring...and flowers
of fire in the night...a palace of icy flowers,
glowing statues and incandescent seas, con-
tinents blazing in the night, in oceans of
snow!...joy...Fullness...emptiness...hope-
less hope.

This image of clarity and light (the "magic city")
is more fully developed in the "radiant city" of The
Killer. Now, instead of a heavy mass sinking deeper and

122

deeper, Choubert begins rising higher and higher
about to "take off" toward "escape." Interestingly
Madeleine and the detective strenuously object that
Choubert is evading his duty. Still, Choubert rises
higher and higher in the air.

> Choubert: The air I breath is lighter than
> air. I am lighter than air. The sun's melting
> into light....I can float through solid objects.
> All forms have disappeared. I'm going up and
> up...shimmering light...I can fly.

But then he loses his nerve ("Oh!...I don't dare") and
falls back heavily to earth again. Choubert cannot completely withdraw from his social conformity and the
social obligation which goes along with it.

> Detective: You...forget yourself, forget
> your duty. That's your great fault. You're
> either too heavy or too light.

The image of flying through air as a symbol of lightness
is taken up again in Amédée and A Stroll in the Air,
while the proliferation image is carried forward in
Victims of Duty by Madeleine's strangely multiplying
teacups and by the endless quantities of bread the detective stuffs into Choubert's mouth, an interesting
image also of the mindless "swallowing" of social
conventions, as well as the effort simply to shut
Choubert up.

In the third group of plays Ionesco concentrates on
the transition between heavy and light. In The Killer
the play moves from light to heavy; in Amédée the movement is from heavy to light. The Killer, 1957, one of
Ionesco's best efforts, was adapted from an earlier
short story "The Photograph of the Colonel." In the
play Berenger accidentally wanders into a marvellous
section of the city which he has never seen before, the
radiant city." It is dazzling, light, airy and beautiful. The architect of the radiant city shows Berenger
around, with the assistance of Dany, the architect's
secretary who soon becomes Berenger's lover. To get
an idea of the visual effect of the radiant city, we
might look at Ionesco's stage directions for the set.

> Atmosphere for Act I will be created by the
> lighting only. At first...the light is grey,
> like a dull November day....Then, suddenly,
> the stage is brilliantly lit; a very bright,
> very white light; just this whiteness, and

also the dense vivid blue of the sky...the
blue, the white, the silence and the empty
stage should give a strange impression of
peace.

To Berenger the city is perfect; it is the outward
manifestation of his life-long hopes and dreams, something he always suspected but was never sure could
really exist.

Berenger: I knew that somewhere in our dark
and dismal city...there was one [district] that
was bright and beautiful...with...sunny
streets and avenues bathed in light....This
radiant city within a city.

Throughout his life Berenger had found a contradiction
between what he felt within himself and what he discovered in the world outside himself. Word and object,
thought and reality never coincided; the external world
never supported his internal vision. In short, Berenger
has always suffered the heaviness of absurdity as
symbolized in the ugly and brutal city surrounding the
radiant district. But now within the radiant city he
finds the perfect coincidence of thought and reality,
inner and outer, the synthesis of essence and existence
which Aristotle recognized as necessary to a meaningful world and which the Romantics tried in vain to
recapture after the collapses of the medieval world
view.

Berenger: To project this universe within
some outside help is needed; some kind of
material, physical light....Gardens, blue sky,
or the spring, which corresponds to the universe
inside and offers a chance of recognition,
which is like a translation or an anticipation
of that universe or a mirror in which its
own smile could be reflected...in which it can
find itself again and say: that's what I am in
reality and I'd forgotten, a smiling being in
a smiling world....Come to think of it, it's
quite wrong to talk of a world within and a
world without, separate world; there's an
initial impulse, of course, which starts from
us, and when it can't project itself, when it
can't fulfill itself objectively, when there's
not total agreement between myself inside and
myself outside, then it's a catastrophe, a
universal contradiction, a schism.

124

The radiant city is, of course, the euphoric vision of emptiness Ionesco reports having experienced in adolescence. In an interesting monologue Berenger relates an almost identical childhood experience to the architect.

Berenger: Suddenly the joy became more intense, breaking all bounds!....The light grew more and more brilliant....My own peace and light spread in their turn throughout the world, I was filling the universe with a kind of ethereal energy....Everything was a virgin, purified, discovered anew...surprise...yet...familiar.... I'm sure I could have flown away, I'd lost so much weight,...I was overcome with the immense sadness you feel at a moment of tragic and intolerable separation...and I felt lost among all those people, all those things.

But if the city is so perfect, Berenger cannot understand why no one is living there. Just as Berenger's (and Ionesco's) childhood experience of evanescent, euphoric emptiness always reverts back to leaden heaviness, so there is something within the radiant city which chokes its light and weighs it down. And this, of course, is the killer, a homicidal maniac who lures his victims by showing them a photograph of the colonel.

After Dany falls prey to the killer, Berenger sets out to track him down. As in the absurdist mystery technique discussed earlier, Berenger follows many false leads through ugly city images of darkness, angry mobs, political harangues until quite by accident he stumbles onto the killer who kills Berenger. Throughout, heaviness is effectively represented by brutal images of city life--darkness, confusion, violence and aggression. Through a striking series of images the play presents the clear progression of light to heaviness, the final inability of lightness to maintain itself. By presenting a sustained image of lightness in the first act, the play suggests a solution to the heaviness of absurdity, a solution nonetheless negated by the presence of the killer who spoils the radiant city.

The first play to move in the opposite direction, toward that solution, is Amédée, or How to Get Rid of It, 1953. Like Choubert, Amédée is a playwright, who has written only one line, however, in fifteen years of a play about an old man and woman (cf. The Chairs). The problem Amédée and his wife, Madeleine, face is how to

125

get rid of an enormous corpse which is mysteriously
growing and spreading out in all directions, threatening
to push them out of their small apartment. It is not
clear how he died, but there is a suggestion of murder
or violence, possibly performed by Amédée himself, whose
"dead" marriage he feels responsible for, which,
combined with the proliferating corpse, poses a striking
image of absurd heaviness. The image of proliferating
matter is strengthened by the burgeoning mushrooms which
sprout all over the apartment. In Point of Departure
Ionesco explains how the theme of proliferating matter
is an image of the dead materiality of objects stripped of human meanings.

> Words, obviously devoid of magic, are replaced
> by accessories, by objects. Countless mushrooms
> sprout in the apartment of the characters
> Amédée and Madeleine; a corpse, stretches with
> 'geometric progression,' also grows there,
> turning out the occupants. In Victims of Duty
> hundreds of cups are piled up to serve coffee
> to three people; the furniture in the New
> Occupant [i.e., The New Tenant], after blocking
> the staircase of the apartment building...,
> ends up by burying the character who wanted
> to settle in the apartment; in The Chairs...
> dozens of chairs, with invisible guests, fill
> the stage; in Jacques [Jack] several noses
> grow on the face of a young girl.[42]

Other images of heaviness we have seen are those of
confomity, brutality and fatigue, which, in addition to
the student in The Lesson, Amédée also expresses in the
first act. "I feel so tired, so tired...worn out,
heavy."

Amédée finally agrees to take the corpse out at
midnight and get rid of it. To pass the time until then
Amédée begins pulling in images through the window by an
invisible rope, and as he does, the characters both
fall into a hypnotic revery which transforms them into
their opposites, Amédée II, who dreams of lightness,
and Madeleine II, who meditates on heaviness. This
is another of Ionesco's experiments with breaking down
the Aristotelian unity of character.

> Amédée II: If only you wished....Nature would
> be so bountiful...wings on our feet, our limbs
> like wings...our shoulders wings...gravity
> abolished...no more weariness.

126

Madeleine II: Night...always night...alone in the world!

Amédée II: An insubstantial universe...
Freedom...Ethereal power...Balance...airy
abundance...world without weight....You could
lift the world with one hand.

Now the roles are reversed, Amédée is himself again,
returning to the reflection of heaviness, while Madeleine
II takes up the lightness revery of Amédée II.

Amédée (himself): Time is heavy. The world
dense.

Madeleine II: Stone is just space. Walls are
void. There is nothing...nothing...

Then the roles begin to reverse yet again.

Amédée: It's heavy. Yet it's so badly stuck
together....Nothing but holes...the walls
are tottering, the leaden mass subsides!

Amédée II: We love each other. We are happy.
In a house of glass, a house of light.

Madeleine II: He means a house of brass,
brass...house of night.

As Amédée prepares to remove the body, light pours
in through the windows and Amédée's spirits are lifted.

Amédée: Look, Madeleine...all the acacia
trees are aglow. Their blossoms are bursting
open and shooting up to the sky. The full-
blown moon is flooding the Heavens with
light, a _living_ planet....He [the corpse]
won't be able to see all this....And space,
space, infinite space!

On the stage the enormous corpse is an ideal image
of leaden heaviness, its sheer bulk resisting all efforts
of human will to budge it and, more important, priva-
tively calling to mind in the strongest terms, as do the
chairs, the absence of the living, breathing, active
person. There is also a suggestion of violence and
brutality in the cause of death and of an amorphous,
unresolved guilt.

As Amédée drags the massive corpse through the

apartment and out into the street the corpse begins to open out like a balloon, rising above the ground carrying Amedee up into the sky. Notice how Ionesco describes this scene in his stage directions.

> (Suddenly a surprising thing happens. The body wound around Amédée's waist seems to have opened out like a sail or a huge parachute; the dead man's head can be seen appearing above the rear wall, and Amédée's head can be seen appearing above the rear wall, drawn up by the parachute....Amédée is flying up and out of reach of the policeman.)

All of this is, of course, extremely difficult to stage and requires a great deal of imagination and technical assistance. Like Lewis Carroll, Ionesco often creates his most striking images by converting puns and idiomati forms of ordinary speech into concrete physical reality. "fishing for thoughts," "going deeper into the recesses of our minds," "feeling high," "swallowing social conventions," "a dead marriage," "a skeleton in the closet." Since dreams also accomplish this, the actual dramatization of these images on stage has the vivid, surreal impact of dreams, especially the well-nigh universal dream of flying, or walking on air, which, just as in most of Ionesco's plays, usually ends by falling back to earth again.

Amédée describes the weight he has lost, which enables him to soar above the city, as his "responsibility," and, as in Victims of Duty, those on the ground including his wife, Madeleine, and the authority figure of the policeman, plead with him to return to his filia and civic duties. But in Amédée the central character at last succeeds in transcending the heavy weight of absurdity toward its mystical lightness.

In his latest group of plays Ionesco is concerned with the tremendous effort required to cut the ties that bind us to the dead, heavy earth and release us into the bright, pure atmosphere of light Ionesco sees as ma only hope. Though the solution to the heaviness of absurdity is clear and is apparently simply a matter of our willing it ("If only you wished)), enormous forces of social and worldly pressure militate against it, making it difficult to achieve for more than a fleeting moment.

Like Beckett's Endgame, which we will discuss in the next chapter, Exit the King (English translation

1963) deals with the problem of how to give up, finally
and completely, as Berenger, Amédée and Choubert have
tried unsuccessfully, all those links to the naive
world we have constructed through human projection, a
world we realize is our own construction (and "so
badly stuck together") and a world we know is responsible
for the dark, heavy side of life, but one we nonetheless
cling to as our most familiar and comfortable refuge.
In Exit the King the image for this effort to relinquish
our tenacious hold on the world is the King's reluctance
to die.

In some old notes for the play, not actually incorporated in the final version, the Queen states this
theme very clearly.

Queen: How could you get so rooted in this
world? You cling to it...you dig your nails
into these clouds, this unreal stuff which you
take for reality, for rock. You see, it's
...breaking up it's dissolving into clouds,
flakes, snow, water, steam, smoke. You cling
to it. Try to loosen your hold, little by
little....Break the habit of living. How
could you forget that all this is just a brief
passage.[43]

As human beings, we project our human concerns upon
the world, but we are not ordinarily aware that we are
doing so. As a result our projected meanings become
objectified, externalized, attaching to objects and we
read our own meanings and significances into the external world around us. This is what draws us to the world,
and makes it an interesting, intelligible, familiar
place, and finally ties us to it. Because of this
projection, the world is perceived, not only as meeting
our needs, but more importantly as thwarting those needs.
Thus, the anthrocentricity of our world-view leads to
unhappiness. So long as a comfortable anthropomorphism
can be maintained, the satisfaction of needs is seen to
exceed or at least balance the ways in which those needs
can be thwarted, but when, in the experience of absurdity,
thought and desire separate from reality and that comfortable world-view begins to break up, as ours has
been for the past several hundred years, all that remains
is the hope without the fulfillment, seeing the world
anthropomorphically as failing or refusing to satisfy
man's deepest needs. The solution, therefore, lies,
not in looking for something in reality to meet our
desires, but in giving up entirely that anthropomorphic

view in which the world is seen as neither meeting nor failing to meet those needs.

By realizing our projecting nature we see the distinction of word and object, thought and reality, which we have defined as absurdity, and this makes it possible to disengage ourselves from our particular socially inform ed view of the world, and indeed from any view of the worl as absolutely coinciding with reality. It is now possible to see reality as utterly transcending all human values, meanings, interests and concerns. But it is not, unfortunately, quite as easy as all that, since our entire biolog cal and social natures rebel against it, and so the King hangs on, wanting to let go but not quite able to do so.

In a clear reference to the crisis of absurdity referred to above, the play opens in a state of natural and political disaster. The country is in chaos; something must be done. The Doctor to the King expresses the general setting of the play, "Yesterday evening it was spring....Now it's November." Berenger, the King, whom we already know from earlier plays to have some autobiographical links to Ionesco, has lost all power over his subjects and indeed over his own body. He is dying. To his politically ambitious first wife, Marguerite, this is interpreted simply in terms of an irreversible loss of personal and political power which the King must now realistically accept. To his more loving second wife, Marie, this is an opportunity for a positive affirmation of detachment from the world of human projection. As in Amédée and Victims of Duty the problem of relinquishing our hold on the conventionally projected world is expressed in terms of social responsibility and power. His death thus represents both the loss of power and his own personal fulfillment, and his wives present him with these two alternatives. Marguerite is a pessimist and a realist who, seeing no ultimate solution, advises Berenger to accept the inevitable loss of the only values in life, power over oneself, others, the world. Marie is an optimist and an idealist who urges the King toward a radical break with this world. Interestingly, Berenger, can choose between these two possibilities. As in Amédée, the difficulty of the solution, ironically, is not made easier by the fact that it is simply a matter of choosing. Within the play it is Marie who speaks most eloquently, and most philosophically.

> Marie (to King): Stop torturing yourself!
> "Exist" and "die" are just words, figments
> of your imagination. Once you realize that,

130

nothing can touch you. Forget your empty
clichés. We can never know what it really
means, "exist" or "die"...Now you exist,
you are. Forget the rest. That's the only
truth. Just be an eternal question mark...
And remember: that you can't find the
answer is an answer in itself...Dive into
an endless maze of wonder and surprise, then
you too will have no end, and can exist
forever. Everything is strange and indefinable. Let it dazzle and confound you!...
Escape from definitions and you will breathe
again!

Open the flood gates of joy and light to
dazzle and confound you. Illuminating
waves of joy will fill your veins with
wonder.

You found that fiery radiance within you.
If it was there once, it is still there
now. Find it again. Look for it in
yourself.

The striking resemblance to mystical, and particularly
Buddhist religious language is no accident. Mystics have
always regarded the meaninglessness of the world as a
solution, rather than a problem. Our problems in life,
according to the mystic, are all due to out attachment to
objects which results from confusing word and object,
mistaking the pointing finger for the moon to which it
points, in the famous Zen epigram. By realizing that
confusion, knowing that thought and reality, mind and
object are ultimately distinct, attachment can be termin-
ated, resulting in a joyous, euphoric state of freedom
and release. In Conversations with Eugene Ionesco,
Ionesco acknowledges a considerable debt to mystic writers,
who "rejected the physical world with all its brightness,
its colour and light, what remains paradoxically is light,
brightness, vividness."[44] From this religious point of
view, the confusion of word and object which causes our
unhealthy attachments to the world spring from the
projection of our own wishes, desires, aims and purposes
onto the world. In Fragments of a Journal Ionesco
discusses the role of desire.

Desire is the most serious obstacle to our
deliverance. Freudianism can thus, to some
extent, be reconciled with Buddhism. Not
with Zen, for to wish to free oneself is

131

still a form of will one should seek to free
oneself from wishing...If we succeeded in
shedding light on Desire...then Desire would
disappear. If we could learn the real
reasons for our reasons, there would no longer
be any reasons for anything. All knots would
be slackened, we would surrender ourselves and
lapse into indifference and nothingness.
Indifference would moreover, allow us to live,
that's to say it might make life less unendur-
able. Not longing to live, not longing to die,
just letting things drift. Zen, as a metaphysical "couldn't-care-less" attitude.[45]

We will see this Buddhist conception of a solution more
fully developed in Beckett.

The same theme of flying above the earth into empty
lightness is taken up again in A Stroll in the Air (1963
The central character is again Berenger, again a writer.
He has come with his wife, Josephine, and daughter, Mart
to a cottage in the English countryside for a holiday.
For the intellectual the last hold on the world is the
desire to wrap it all up in a verbal formula, to talk
about heaviness, emptiness, the absurdity of life. The
last thing to be seen as absurd is the theory of absurdity. In the play Berenger is tired of trying to explain
everything in words; and he wishes to be released from
this compulsion.

Berenger: I've always known I never had any
reason to write...Once upon a time, though
I'm really a nihilist, there was some strange
force inside me that made me...write. I can't
go on any longer...For years it was a consolation
to me to be able to say there was nothing to say.
But now I feel far too sure I was right...writing
isn't a game for me any more...It ought to lead
to something else, but it doesn't.

The play's first image of the transparent, empty lightness to be sought by way of escape is the "anti-world",
the opposite and negation of our ordinary, mundane
world which in the other plays has been challenged and
bracketed by the dislocation of language. In the anti-
world objects appear and disappear from within "the void
Berenger and Marthe see it; his wife, Josephine, does
not. As in several of the earlier plays, in particular
Victims of Duty, it is the wife who, along with authority
figures, like the professor, detective, fireman, policeman, emperor, king, represent an insistence upon conform-

132

ity to social obligations which tie us to the heaviness of absurdity and work against release. Not all women play this heavy role, however, witness Marie and Marthe.

As in Amédée and Victims of Duty, to see the anti-world, like the experience of lightness generally, is to a large extent an act of personal will.

> Berenger: There's no proof that it exists, but
> when you think about it, you can find it in
> your own thoughts. The evidence is in your
> mind. There's not just one Anti-world. There
> are several...universes, and they're all
> interlocking.

The anti-world is an image of the humanly creative construction of particular world views from different interested human perspectives. All of these views come from "the void" in the sense that reality in itself transcends all those conceptual and linguistic forms which give our interpreted world its discernible shape and pattern. Reality is void, not like an empty bag, but empty of linguistic and conceptual distinctions and demarcations.

> Berenger: And to think there are people who
> imagine the void is like a huge black hole,
> a bottomless pit: and yet the void is neither
> black nor white and to be bottomless, it would
> need acres and acres and acres of space...The void
> is neither white nor black, it doesn't exist,
> it's everywhere.

The void is simply the transcendence of reality from linguistic boundaries. Compare this statement of Ionesco with that of the great 9th century Zen master, Huang-po, in his discussion of the void.

> Men are afraid to forget their own minds, fearing
> to fall through the void with nothing on to which
> they can cling. They do not know that the void
> is not really the void but the real realm of
> things.
>
> Though basically everything is without objective
> existence, you must not come to think of anything
> nonexistent, and though things are not nonexistent
> you must not form a concept of anything existing.
> For "existence" and "nonexistence" are both
> empirical concepts no better than illusions.

> [Reality] is neither long nor short, big nor
> small, for it transcends all limits, measures,
> names, traces and comparisons. It is that
> which you see before you -- begin to reason
> about it and at once you fall into error. It
> is like the boundless void which cannot be
> fathomed or measured.
>
> So let your symbolic conception be that of a
> void...Eschew all symbolizing whatever, for by
> this eschewal, is "symbolized" the Great Void
> in which is neither unity nor multiplicity --
> that Void which is not really void, that Symbol
> which is not a symbol.[46]

It is interesting but not really surprising to find in t
revolutionary 20th century theory of absurdity significa
parallels with some of the most ancient philosophical
thought both East and West.

As Berenger experiences the joy of this emptying
experience and the sense of novelty at the fresh reality
revealed thereby, he begins to walk on air, at first onl
a few feet above the ground, but then soaring high above
the English hillsides and village, his wife pleading wit
him all this while to be sensible and walk on the ground
like everyone else. To Berenger it's as though he is
returning to an earlier experience which he had almost
forgotten.

> Berenger: I've never been so relaxed; I've
> never felt so happy. I've never felt so light,
> so weightless...When I look around me, it's
> as though I was seeing everything for the first
> time. As though I'd just been born...Like some
> feeling of joy that's been forgotten yet still
> familiar, like something that's belonged to me
> from the beginning of time. You lose it every-
> day and yet it's never really lost. And the
> proof is that you can find it again...It's all
> very concrete...a sort of divine intoxication.

The need to "fly", as well as the ability to fly, is not
an extraordinary quirk of the half-insane, but part of
the inmost nature of all human beings. As the Buddhists
say, the Buddha-nature is the true nature of everyone
whether he or she knows it or not. The reason most of
us are not aware of it is that we forget our true nature

> Berenger: Man has a crying need to fly...It's
> as necessary and as natural as breathing...

134

everyone knows how to fly. It's an innate
gift, but everyone forgets...It would be better
for us to starve than not to fly. I expect
that's why we feel so unhappy.

In one sense it is very easy; all that is really required
is the desire.

   Berenger: "It's perfectly simple. All you need is
the will to do it." In another sense, however, it is
exceedingly difficult.   Reflecting on all the darkness,
injustice, cruelty of the human social order, Berenger,
like Choubert, loses faith and falls back to earth "sad,"
"depressed," and "deflated."

   In his latest published work to be translated into
English, a novel called The Hermit (1974), Ionesco returns
to the light-heavy experience with which it all began 25
years earlier.

   Joy was suddenly realizing, in a way I might
   describe as supernatural, that the world is
   there, that you are there in the world, that
   one exists, that I exist. Now everything
   seemed to prove the inexistence of things
   and my own existence. I was afraid of
   disappearing...I had the impression that the
   little seismic disturbances, imperceptible
   but fairly numerous, had made the world
   extremely fragile. Everything was disintegrat-
   ing, everything seemed on the verge of sinking
   into an ordinary void. The universe where
   reality was less and less resistant...I felt
   my self teetering in a world about to topple.
   Strange how everything is simultaneoulsy so
   present and so absent, so hard so thick, and
   so fragile...The nausea of nothingness. And
   then the nausea of surfeit...I walked down the
   street...touching the walls, simultaneously
   fearing that they might crush me or that they
   might vanish.[47]

There was a kind of trembling in the walls and
ceiling that surrounded me, luminous vibrations
in the blinding light. The walls and the roof
seemed to be breaking up; their lines became
blurred. They lost their density and seemed to
me to turn into something increasingly transparent,
penumbras, evanescent shadows...Then I saw them
shrivel up and slowly recede into the distance.
They melted like so much transparent smoke into
the luminous distance, then disappeared. Before

my eyes, the desert stretched, vast beneath the
brilliant sky, the burning sun, to the very
horizon. There was no longer anything but sand
sparkling in the light. My room seemed to be
suspended, silent, a tiny dot in all the
immensity...Now the wall disappeared in turn...
Where the wall had been images began to form
and slowly reform. It grew very bright...A
long pathway. At the end, a light brighter than
daylight. The light came nearer, encompassing
everything. How could my room contain it?[48]

Chapter Four: References

1. Eugene Ionesco, "The Point of Departure", Leonard C. Pronko, trans., in _Theatre Arts_, June 1958, p. 17.

2. Ionesco, _Fragments of a Journal_, Jean Stewart, trans. (London: Faber and Faber, 1976), pp. 41-42.

3. _Ibid._, pp. 129-130.

4. Ionesco, _Conversations with Eugene Ionesco_, transcribed by Claude Bonnefoy, Jan Dawson, trans. (New York: Holt, Rinehart, and Winston, 1971), p. 122.

5. Ionesco, _Fragments of a Journal_, op. cit., pp. 74-75.

6. Ionesco, _Conversations with Eugene Ionesco_, op. cit., p. 61.

7. _Ibid._

8. _Ibid._, p. 62.

9. _Ibid._, p. 93.

10. _Ibid._, p. 114.

11. Ionesco, _Fragments of a Journal_, op. cit., p. 83.

12. Ionesco, "Dialogues avec Ionesco," transcribed by Lerminier, in Richard N. Coe, _Ionesco_ (London: Oliver and Boyd, 1961), p. 73.

13. Ionesco, _Fragments of a Journal_, op. cit.

14. Ionesco, _Conversations with Eugene Ionesco_, op. cit., p. 157.

15. _Ibid._, pp. 120-121.

16. Ionesco, _Present Past, Past Present_, Helen Lane, trans. (New York: Grove Press, 1971), p. 169.

17. _Ibid._, pp. 169-170.

18. _Ibid._, p. 191.

19. Ionesco, _Conversations with Eugene Ionesco_, op. cit., p. 123.

20. Alain Robbe-Grillet, "From Realism to Reality," in _For A New Novel_, Richard Howard, trans. (New York: Grove Press, 1965), p. 166.

21. Ionseco, _Fragments of a Journal_, op, cit., p. 30.

22. Ionesco, _Present Past, Past Present_, op. cit., p. 139.

23. Ionesco, _Fragments of a Journal_, op. cit., p. 61.

24. _Ibid._, p. 62

25. Ionesco, _Present Past, Past Present_, op. cit., p. 131.

26. Ionesco, _Fragments of a Journal_, op. cit., pp. 129-30.

27. Ionesco, _Present Past, Past Present_, op. cit., pp. 150-51.

28. _Ibid._

29. _Ibid._, pp. 171-72.

30. _Ibid._, p. 154.

31. _Ibid._, p. 157.

32. Ionesco, _Conversations with Eugene Ionesco_, op. cit., pp. 123-24.

33. Ionesco, _Fragments of a Journal_, op. cit., p. 40

34. _Ibid._, p. 20.

35. _Ibid._, p. 40.

36. _Ibid._, p. 41.

37. Ionesco, "The Point of Departure," op. cit., p. 18.

38. Ionesco, _Fragments of a Journal_, op. cit., p. 18.

39. Ionesco, _Conversations with Eugene Ionesco_, op. cit., p. 128.

40. _Ibid._, p. 73.

41. Ionesco, letter to Sylvain Dhomme, in Martin Esslin, _The Theatre of the Absurd_ (Harmondsworth, England: Penguin Books, 1968), p. 100.

42. Ionesco, "The Point of Departure," _op. cit._

43. Ionesco, _Fragments of a Journal_, _op. cit._, p.44.

44. Ionesco, _Conversations with Eugene Ionesco_, _op. cit._, p. 42.

45. Ionesco, _Fragments of a Journal_, _op. cit._, p. 51.

46. Huang-Po, _The Teaching of Huang-Po_, John Blofeld, trans. (New York: Grove Press, 1959).

47. Ionesco, _The Hermit_, Richard Seaver, trans. (New York: Viking Press, 1974), pp. 94-95.

48. _Ibid._, pp. 168-69.

CHAPTER 5: BECKETT

Among the writers considered in this book, Beckett
is the most singleminded and consistent in his determination to overcome the tragic heaviness of absurdity.
Unlike the other absurdists, this is the only theme we
find in all of his writing from his earliest publication
in 1930 to his most recent work. He is also, surprisingly perhaps, the most optimistic about the possibility
of finally breaking through to the euphoric light side
of absurdity. Because this requires, as we saw in
Ionesco, transcending all forms of conventional understanding, including linguistic conventions, Beckett is
without doubt the most difficult of all the absurdists
to understand. Even more than Ionesco, Beckett's
message is conveyed through the peculiarities of his
linguistic medium; content is revealed through form.
Since that message is, above all, the desirability of
dismantling all habitual, familiar patterns of thought,
Beckett's writing style is anything but ordinary.

Those unfamiliar with Beckett's prose works will
be surprised, I think, by his long-term, persistent
interest in what may be called the philosophy of resign-
ation--a philosophical position articulated by those
writers of the past with whom Beckett has expressed the
strongest affinity, viz., Schopenhauer, the ancient
Stoics, and Eastern, especially Hindu and Buddhist
philosophers. This philosophical bent appears as early
as 1931 when Beckett's remarkable study of Proust first
appeared in print.

In this book, which predates Beckett's stylistic
experiments with language, Beckett offers an interpretation
of Proust from the standpoint of Schopenhauer in a way
which reveals much about Beckett's own intellectual
orientation. What Beckett has done in Proust is to
interpret Proust's concern with the effects of time upon
the individual's consciousness of the world in terms of
Schopenhauer's theory of Will. According to Schopenhauer,
our customary patterns of thought and perception, which
are rooted in our biological, instinctual nature,
structure the world as we know it and demarcate ourselves from it. Nonetheless, Schopenhauer argues, this
is an illusion which can be overcome only by an enormous

141

rejection of all our deepest instincts, replacing our very will to survive by a detached, disinterested aesthetic perception of an ideal reality transcending all linguistic and conceptual distinctions.

Although the terminology varies, the idea, rooted in Kant's transcendental idealism, is basically the same as we found in Camus, Sartre, and Ionesco. The ordinary world of our awareness is a world structured by human consciousness and rooted in a sense of time and purposeful activity. Because of the success of this mutual accommodation of thought and object, we are not normally aware of our projection of interests and desires upon the world, and so, through habit and memory we take this anthropomorphized version of the world for reality itself, confusing word and object, essence and existence, and this contributes to our sense of comfortable familiarity with the world--which eventually leads to boredom. Nonetheless, we are not always so totally unaware of our creative efforts in the construction of our view of the world. In all those ways in which absurdity enters human experience, we can and do become aware of the projecting nature of human thought and when this occurs, word and object, thought and reality, become detached from one another. In the brief transition from one acceptable construction to another, the usual comforting sense of familiarity, bordering on boredom, turns to suffering. Time, Habit, Memory, Boredom, and Suffering--these, then, are the technical terms of Beckett's analysis.

> Habit is a compromise effected between the
> individual and his environment, or between the
> individual and his own organic eccentricities,
> the guarantee of a dull inviolability....Habit
> is the ballast that chains the dog to his
> vomit....Life is a succession of habits,
> since the individual is a succession of
> individuals; the world being a projection
> of the individual's consciousness (an object-
> ification of the individual's will, Schopenhauer
> would say), the pact must be continually re-
> newed....The creation of the world did not
> take place once and for all time, but takes
> place every day. Habit then is the generic
> term for the countless treatises concluded
> between the countless subjects that constitute
> the individual and their countless correlative
> objects. The periods of transition that
> separate consecutive adaptations...represent
> the perilous zones in the life of the

individual,...when for a moment the boredom
of living is replaced by the suffering of
being.[1]

Here Beckett takes the realist side of Sartre and Camus
against the phenomenological idealism of Heidegger and
Husserl. Despite our customary forgetfulness of projection ("Habit") which tends to equate reality with
humanly interpreted reality, we occasionally become
aware that thought and reality are distinct and thus
cognizant of the fact that existence is not coincident
with essence, but transcends all human categories.

The above passage is also reminiscent of Ionesco's
analysis of the delicate balance in meaningful discourse
between the complete transparency of naive projection
and the disturbing opacity of original insight. If
we speak entirely our own language, no one can understand us; if we speak entirely the language of others,
we are untrue to our own unique insights.

Either we speak and act for ourselves--in
which case speech and action are distorted and
emptied of their meaning by an intelligence
that is not ours, or else we speak and
act for others--in which case we speak and act
a lie.[2]

Despite the effect of Habit, we are not totally
abosrbed in conventional cliches and can and do, therefore, originate fresh, individual perspectives which
open up new dimensions of the world more adequately
reflecting our own individual points of view. But this
new perspective, which appears so exciting and creative
at first, quickly degenerates, as Ionesco saw, into a
familiar, publicly accepted convention. So, the "treaty"
or "adaptation" of self to world moves in a series of
transitions between opaque awareness of itself (which
is Suffering) and a naively transparent forgetfulness
of self (which is Habit).

The fundamental duty of Habit...consists in a
perpetual adjustment and readjustment of our
organic sensibility to the conditions of its
worlds. Suffering represents the omission of
that duty..., and boredom its adequate performance. The pendulum oscillates between these
two terms: Suffering--that opens a window on
the real and is the main condition of the
artistic experience, and Boredom--...[3]

143

Most of the time we are victims of Habit, interpreting every object in our experience, including ourselves, as falling neatly within a familiar human category. The object before us, to recall Sartre's examples
from Nausea, is simply a glass of beer, a tree root,
a streetcar seat. Since these categories are our own
inventions, it is comforting to see the world conform to
these familiar classifications, as Camus points out in
The Myth of Sisyphus. But since we only see things
thereby in terms of their general essence, as examples
of certain kinds or types of thing, we never experience,
in ordinary circumstances, the existing reality of the
object we so blithely classify. We see its "essence"
but not its "existence," its generality, but not its
individuality. But when, occasionally, for one reason
or another, we are confronted with an object which
refuses to be classified, we see the "naked Reality"
of this unique individual transcending all conceptual
classifications and, in Sartre's technical language,
begin painfully to "exist."

Beckett offers several interesting illustrations
from Proust of the alternating wonder of reality once th
customary conceptual mask of Habit has fallen from it,
and the opposite state in which the marvellous slips
into the mundane. The first, reminiscent of Sartrean
nausea, occurs when the child in Proust's story enters
an unfamiliar hotel room.

> There is no room for his body in this vast and
> hideous apartment, because his attention has
> peopled it with gigantic furniture, a storm
> of sound and an agony of colour. Habit has not
> had time to silence the explosions of the clock,
> reduce the hostility of the violet curtains,...
> Alone in this room that is not yet a room but
> cavern of wild beasts, invested on all sides
> by the implacable strangers whose privacy he has
> disturbed, he desires to die.[4]

But when he enters the same room a second time, the
reverse experience takes place.

> He arrives tired and ill, as on the former
> occasion....Now, however, the dragon has been
> reduced to docility, and the cavern is a
> room....Already will, the will not to suffer,
> Habit, having recovered from its momentary
> paralysis, has laid the foundations of its
> evil and necessary structure, and the vision...

begins to fade and to lose that miraculous
relief and clarity that no effort of deliberate rememoration can impart or restore.[5]

In Beckett's view the loss of Habit is not totally
without reward, however, and indeed, is the ultimate
key to freedom from Suffering.

> The old ego dies hard. Such as it was, a
> minister of dullness, it was also an agent of
> security. When it ceases to perform that
> second function, when it is opposed by a
> phenomenon that it cannot reduce to the con-
> dition of a comfortable and familiar concept,
> when, in a word, it betrays its trust as a
> screen to spare its victim the spectacle of
> reality, it disappears, and the victim, now
> an ex-victim, for a moment free, is exposed
> to that reality--exposure that has its ad-
> vantages and disadvantages.[6]

Here we notice a crucial ambiguity in Beckett's account
very much like the ambiguity we saw in Sartre's notion
of a "naked Reality." Do we, in the absurd experience,
actually see reality as it is in itself, or do we
simply realize that reality transcends our conceptualizations? The first position is, as we have seen,
untenable on the absurdist's own argument for the separation of word and object, essence and existence.
Unfortunately it is easy to confuse the two positions,
as Beckett appears to have done in this early formulation. This is closely tied, as we will see shortly,
with Beckett's use of the idealist language of Schopenhauer
which holds out the promise of a veridical alternative
to the illusion of ordinary projection.

As Sartre and Ionesco also perceived, stripped of
its familiar conceptual garb, the object appears fresh
and new, as though seen for the very first time, and
absolutely unique and individual. Borrowing Schopenhauer's
unusual and somewhat confusing language, borrowed in
turn from Kant, Beckett contrasts the general conceptual
classification of sense impressions in everyday cognition with the direct intuition of the unique essence
or "Idea" of the concrete individual itself. In the
Critique of Pure Reason Kant distinguished the Concepts
of the Understanding by which we classify things as
they appear to us in sense experience from the Ideas
of Reason which include such things as the soul, God
and the world as a whole, of which there is no sense
experience. For Kant the Ideas were merely "regulative;"

that is, they did not designate real entities which we could understand or know existed. They were simply notions which we needed in order to understand the world as we do. Since conceptual understanding was limited by Kant to things as they _appear_ to us in sense experience and Ideas were merely regulative, Kant's philosophy was left with the unhappy consequence that there is no knowledge or even understanding of reality itself. It made sense to talk about a reality transcending human thought, but just because it did transcend human ways of thinking, it could not be thought or described.

This proved to be too much for Kant's Idealist successors, Fichte, Hegel, Schelling, and Schopenhauer, who abandoned Kant's critical attitude toward Ideas in favor of a new conception of Ideas as a nonclassificatory way of apprehending reality directly. In German philosophy throughout the 19th century, therefore, classification was limited to mere appearances, while Reality was apprehended in a totally different, if somewhat mysterious way. For Hegel Ideal Reality is the integration of everything into a gigantic contextual whole purposefully evolving through time; for Schopenhauer, on the other hand, the Ideas stand for timeless, eternal, distinct individuals in the Platonic tradition. Like many literary figures of the time, such as Croce and Bergson, Beckett uses Schopenhauer's notion of Idea to represent that direct intuition of individual existence detached from all selfish, practical purposes and desires and in direct contrast to the ordinary, purposeful, practical classification of the individual object into its generic kind or concept.

> But when the object is perceived as particular
> and unique and not merely the member of a
> family, when it appears independent of any
> general notion and detached from the sanity of
> a cause, isolated and inexplicable in the light
> of ignorance, then and then only may it be a
> source of enchantment. Unfortunately Habit
> has laid its veto on this form of perception,
> its action being precisely to hide the essence--
> the Idea--of the object in the haze of concep-
> tion.

As we saw in our investigation of Sartre's _Nausea_, the conceptual boundaries we cognitively impose on objects includes not only the classification of objects into nameable kinds, but the classification of sense impressions into _objects_. As Kant pointed out, "object" is itself a humanly imposed concept. Thus in _Nausea_

146

objects not only become detached from their names, but eventually dissolve into an indiscriminate mist or fog. Somewhat like Hume, Beckett carries this line of reasoning one step further to include the disintegration of the concept of the mental object, the knowing subject or immutable self. This too is a convenient myth no less than the myth of a permanent, stable physical object. Subject and object are both in a constant state of flux, and each is constantly altering and being altered by the other. For Sartre "nausea" and "existence" heighten the awareness of ego; for Beckett such experiences diminish that awareness. Subject and object arise together in the act of projecting the ordinary world of human concerns. As Beckett remarks in an earlier passage above, when that projection ceases the "ego...disappears." For convenience we can consider the object as a permanent entity for a changing subject or, as Beckett prefers in the later fiction, we can consider a permanent self before a changing object. But both are convenient fictions; in reality there is no such thing as a discrete, distinct subject or object.

> So far we have considered a mobile subject
> before an ideal object, immutable and incor-
> ruptible....Exemption from intrinsic flux in
> a given object does not change the fact that
> it is the correlative of a subject that does
> not enjoy such immunity. The observer infects
> the observed with his own mobility.[8]

Since subject and object arise in opposition to one another in a practical, active context of a subject wanting and moving to acquire an object, the key to the projection of a humanly interpreted world is purpose and desire. If the projected world is an illusion, then so is purpose and desire. As such diverse philosophers as Schopenhauer, Heidegger and John Dewey attest, we are basically purposeful creatures, doing one thing for the sake of another. Consequently we perceive things in terms of their ability to meet or thwart our needs and desires. Thus we base our classification of things on their reference to our purposes, and our attitude toward things is consequently interested, selfish and practical. The concept of an object independent of the self appears as the goal of our wants and desires, and the concept of an independent self appears as the source of those desires and of their satisfaction or disappointment. The underlying structure of our view of the world, then, is the notion of an object for the sake of an independent subject. If that is an illusion, then so is the world constructed

147

thereon. Therefore, echoing Schopenhauer and the Hindu
and Buddhist philosophers he endorsed, as well as the
Stoics, Beckett argues that our desire to possess things
is based on an illusion. Either the object changes by
the time we get it or we ourselves have changed.

> No object prolonged in this temporal dimension
> tolerates possession....All that is active,
> all that is time and space, is endowed with
> what might be described as an abstract, ideal
> and absolute impermeability.[9]

It is not that our particular view of things is
mistaken, but that every human perception imposes its
own distortions, even as it reveals new aspects of
reality. There simply is no way of knowing reality as
it is in itself. Thought and reality, essence and
existence, are ultimately distinct and not to be confused with one another. As such, we must take all
conceptualizations, including the concept of a subject
and an object, with a certain "grain of salt." So
far as our understanding is concerned we are locked
within our own minds, imprisoned in a "sealed jar," as
Beckett describes it in the novel, Molloy, internalizing
everything within the self, as Rilke also tried to do.

> The good or evil disposition of the object has
> neither reality nor significance....Such as it
> was, it has been assimilated to the only
> world that has reality and significance, the
> world of our own latent consciousness, and
> its cosmography has suffered a dislocation.[10]

Since the problem springs from the illusion of
accomplishing goals, achieving ends and satisfying
desires, the solution consists in rejecting desire,
that is, in overcoming, or at least seeing through, our
ordinary biological impulse as purposeful, willing
creatures, without which, as we have seen, the construction of our view of the world cannot take place. As
Beckett says, Proust's treatment of Memory and Habit are
those

> flying buttresses of the temple raised to
> commemorate the wisdom of the architect that
> is also the wisdom of all the sages, from
> Brahma to Leopardi, the wisdom that consists
> not in the satisfaction but in the ablation of
> desire.[11]

We eliminate suffering, not by reducing those things

148

which cause us suffering, but by dismantling the willing
ego which makes suffering possible.

> Wisdom consists in obliterating the faculty
> of suffering rather than in a vain attempt
> to reduce the stimuli that exasperate that
> faculty.[12]

In following so strictly the Romantic, Idealist
thought of the 19th century Beckett falls one step
short in this early work of the bliss of emptiness he
achieves in the later works. Assuming that ordinary
forms of thought fail to capture reality as it is in
itself, do we conclude that reality absolutely transcends all forms of thought, or do we hold out the hope
that some other, extraordinary form of thought does
gain direct access to the thing-in-itself? This is
that crucial ambiguity in Beckett's early view we
noticed before, an ambiguity which also infects Sartre's
notion of our perception of a "naked World" in the
experience of absurdity. The Romantic Idealists opt
for the second, as a kind of intermediary step to the
more radical position of the first. Some forms of
thought are illusory, but others may not be so. This
is a comforting assurance, but in principle the same
argument would seem to work for all forms of thought.
Word and object, essence and existence, are never identical; confusing the two is always an illusion. It is
a subtle but crucial move, as we saw earlier, from
the notion that we see a "naked World" to the realization that reality transcends all forms of human
thought. It is one thing to see someone naked; it is
quite another to know that they are wearing clothing.

Later Beckett himself makes that move, but in this
early period he follows Schopenhauer's theory that by
renouncing will and the whole classificatory mechanism
of the understanding, we achieve an aesthetic and
mystical oneness with the essential will-less Idea of
the unique individual. Since desire, the ego-object
distinction and the ordinary projected world form an
inseparable package, rejecting any one of these is
tantamount to rejecting the lot; thus, by renouncing
the naive desire to possess the object, the projected
world dissolves and the ego-object distinction collapses.
Thus we recover, as the Romantics hoped, our lost
synthesis of word and object, thought and reality,
essence and existence, which philosophers have been
trying to reunite since Aristotle's first attempt.
This essentially idealist and romantic notion had an
extraordinary effect on intellectuals in the early part

of this century, including Bergson, Pater, Croce, and
Baudelaire. The ordinary purposeful cognition of the
world creates an ego-object split which alienates us
from the world; while detached, disinterested mystical
and aesthetic perception heals the ego-object split
and reunites us with the object. This is a well-known
concern of early 19th century Romantics, like Coleridge.

> A poet's heart and intellect should be com-
> bined, intimately combined and unified with
> the great appearances of nature.[13]

> [Art is the] reconciler of nature and men. It
> is, therefore, the power of humanizing nature,
> of infusing the thoughts and possessions
> of man into everything which is the object of
> his contemplations,...[and whose object is to]
> make external, internal, the internal external,
> to make nature, thought, and thought nature.[14]

What is not so readily recognized is the impact of
this way of thinking on such "moderns" as Nietzsche,
D.H. Lawrence, and Baudelaire.

> The most characteristic quality of modern
> man; the strange contrast between an inner
> life to which nothing outward corresponds
> and an outward existence unrelated to what is
> within.[15]

> There is nothing of me that is alone and
> absolute except in my mind, and we shall
> find that the mind has no existence by itself;
> it is only the glitter of the sun on the sur-
> face of the waters. So that my individualism
> is really an illusion. I am part of the
> great whole, and I can never escape. But I
> can deny my connections, break them and become
> a fragment. Then I am wretched.[16]

> The eye fixes itself on a tree, harmoniously
> swayed by the wind; in a few seconds that which
> in the brain of the poet would be only a
> completely natural simile becomes a fact.
> In the tree one's passions, longing, or
> melancholy come to life.[17]

This Romantic view continues to be of great importance
in contemporary Gestalt and developmental psychology,
e.g., in Werner, Koffka, Arnheim and Kohler who hold
that the ego-object distinction rises and falls with

goal-directed, purposeful, practical activity. Because
it is disinterested and detached from practical considerations, aesthetic experience transcends the ego-
object distinction.

No doubt the experience referred to is a genuine
one. In aesthetic experience the object does not appear
as something for the sake of some further end which I
need or want; and so I forget myself as a wanting,
desiring ego for a moment and am simply absorbed in the
perception of the object for its own sake. What is
questionable in this analysis is whether this experience should be interpreted as a direct experience of
absolute reality in which ego and object collapse into
One, or whether, as I would prefer to say, putting it
negatively, that there is no longer any conceptual
classification at work, no longer any purposeful opposition of subject and object. We are _released_ from
cognition without thereby acquiring a _new_ cognition.
We are _freed_ of theories of reality, rather than
achieving a _new_ theory of reality.

In _Proust_ Beckett describes this synthesis of
subject and object and the collapse of past, present,
and future, as

> the Paradise that has been lost. The identi-
> fication of immediate with past experience, the
> recurrence of past action or reaction in the
> present, amounts to a participation between
> ideal and the real, imagination and direct
> apprehension, symbol and substance.[18]

Beckett also agrees with Schopenhauer that by overcoming will or purpose, we transcend our sense of time,
and thus of death. As we saw earlier, our sense of
time springs from our sense of purpose. By acting now,
on the basis of remembered past experience, for some
imagined future gain, I structure my world temporally.
Our sense of time, in other words, is tied to our practical, purposive posture toward the world--and rises
and falls with it. In the mystical, aesthetic vision

> the experience is at once imaginative and
> empirical, at once an evocation and direct
> perception, real without being merely actual,
> ideal wthout being merely abstract, the ideal
> real, the essential, the extratemporal. But
> if this mystical experience communicates an
> extratemporal essence, it follows that the
> communicant is for the moment an extratemporal

being. Consequently the Proustian solution
consists...in the negation of Death because
negation of Time. Death is dead because Time
is dead.[19]

This is reminiscent of Roquentin's escape in Nausea from
existence to the timeless, ideal realm of pure essence
as exemplified in mathematical figures, songs, and
stories. So, too, for Beckett, as for Schopenhauer,
as for the Romantics generally, the chief avenue to
this new freedom is art.

So now in the exaltation of his brief eternity,
having emerged from the darkness of time and
habit and passion and intelligence, he understands the necessity of art. For in the brightness of art alone can be deciphered the baffled
ecstasy that he had known before in the in-
scrutable superficies of a cloud, a triangle,
a spire, a flower, a pebble, when the mystery,
the essence, the Idea, imprisoned in matter
(appears)....And he understands the meaning
of Baudelaire's definition of reality as "the
adequate union of subject and object."[20]

He even accepts Schopenhauer's elevation of music to
the highest place among the arts. According to
Schopenhauer, the other arts must approach reality
indirectly through the intermediary of materials taken
from the ordinary spatio-temporal realm of appearances,
that is, through sensory images. Only music can by-
pass this, penetrating directly to the heart of reality.
Because of the ego-object split, it becomes more and
more difficult, within this Romantic framework, to find
an adequate symbol or image from external phenomena
to express the thought within. This is what T.S. Eliot
called the problem of finding the "objective correlative," the problem which, according to Hegel, is the
main motivation behind the shift from Classical to
Romantic Art. The solution to this problem, Hegel
said, was to internalize the image.[21] "External phenomena are no longer able to express this inward life,"
as Hegel said, and this leads to the desire for the kind
of art voiced in Rilke's Duino Elegies, namely, in
Hegel's words, "that mode of expression which is without
externality, invisibly declaring itself, in other words
a form of music simply, which is neither an object nor
possesses form."[22] The idea of music as the ideal art
form towards which all the other arts tend has been
closely associated with Romantic thought from its begin-
nings. Wackenroder, for example, wrote in 1799 that

152

music "shows us all the movement of our spirit, dis-
embodied," and Heine described music as that

> which perhaps aims at nothing less than the
> dissolution of the whole material world....
> Music is perhaps the last word of art... To
> me it is of great significance that Beethoven
> became deaf in the end so that even the in-
> visible world of tones ceased to have any
> resonant reality for him,[23]

a view reminiscent of Keat's poetic statement that
unheard melodies are sweeter than heard ones. Thus the
Romantic, Idealist movement was torn between the desire
to reunite external with internal by internalizing
external (subjective idealism) or reuniting them by
externalizing internal (objective idealism). Ultimately,
neither works for the simple reason that there remains
an external reality which transcends and can therefore
never be completely reconciled with thought. This is
the old problem of reconciling idealism with dualistic
realism.

If we accept the conclusion that linguistic, conceptual thought fails to capture reality as it is in
itself, how _do_ we articulate what that reality _is_? As
Robbe-Grillet found, it is obviously going to be very
difficult to describe linguistically a reality which we
assert to transcend all linguistic description. Here
meaningful conceptual thought and language simply
reach their outer limits. Do we say that since reality
is without linguistic distinctions and demarcations it
is therefore One and Indivisible, or do we simply say,
negatively, that reality is not exhausted in but transcends all linguistic distinctions and demarcations?
The first, chosen by Idealists and Spiritualists,
affirms the existence of a monistic, transcendent
Spriritual Reality behind all appearances, the second,
which the absurdists opt for, asserts that there is
nothing describable or even thinkable behind the humanly
projected world--often symbolized by the concept of
Nothingness, or The Void. At its outer limits, where
ordinary words and concepts have exhausted their customary meanings, apparently contradictory formulations,
like these, are used to express the same position,
and what seem divergent paths arrive at a single destination. Paradoxically both "the One Reality" and "the
Void" become symbols for the same failure of words to
capture reality. What is at stake is ironically, not
a theory of reality at all, but a theory of language,

of how words do and do not relate to reality. In this
early period Beckett uses the Idealist symbol of a
transcendent, monistic reality; later he expresses
himself in the symbols of nothingness.

Although Beckett later abandoned the Idealist
belief in a transcendent Ideal Reality to be grasped in
some noncognitive form of intuition, he clings throughout to the notion that the solution consists in overcoming the illusion of the ordinary world of projected
purpose. Whether there is a positive alternative or
not, this must be rejected.

Beckett's later rejection of Schopenhauer is like
the Buddhist rejection of a single Brahmanic Spiritual
Reality in favor of the Void, or Nothingness. The
ordinary view of the world is an illusion because it
confuses concepts with objects, but no advance is made
by interpreting this insight to mean that we have
gained new knowledge of a new reality where concept
and object finally do coincide. This is simply the
same confusion all over again. It is better to say,
with the Buddhists, that we now know there is no
knowledge of any absolute Reality in this sense. And
the best symbol for this position, assuming we must use
some symbol, is "the Void." Hence instead of gaining
knowledge, we simply give up all attempts to identify
word and object.

This is not a metaphysical theory of reality, but
a statement about the possibility of having a metaphysic
theory of reality. It is not a theory about reality but
a theory about theories. As the great 9th century
Buddhist scholar Nagarjuna put it,

> The Great Sage preached the law of Emptiness
> In order to free men from all views.
> If one still holds the view that Emptiness exists,
> Such a person the Buddhas will not transform.[24]
>
> It cannot be called void or not void,
> Or both or neither;
> But in order to point it out,
> It is called, "the Void."[25]

"Reality" and "Void" are therefore mere symbols of the
mutually transcending relation of word and object,
thought and reality (as are all symbols once we refuse t
identify or confuse them), symbols, in short, of the
euphoric side of absurdity.

154

Instead of acquiring a new view of _reality_ we gain a new insight into the relationship of word and thought to reality, viz, that the two are distinct, each transcending the other, which is precisely what the Buddhists mean by Nothingness, that reality is, as Beckett says some 20 years later, The Unnamable.

In this novel (The Unnamable, 1958) Beckett explores in a stream-of-consciousness monologue the theoretical considerations which underlie the best of his late fiction. The problem which these works address is what alternative we have to the illusion of projection. Can we, for example, reject this in favor of some other, non-illusory approach to reality, as the Idealists urge? But this is impossible, as we have seen; there _is_ no human way to understand reality as it is in itself. Kant was therefore right after all. The illusion of ordinary thought is not that it is mistaken, but that it falsely identifies word and object, essence and existence. But if reality transcends thought, it transcends all human thought, even the most spiritually refined and metaphysically sophisticated. So that won't work.

Perhaps we could simply stop thinking and talking altogether. But this, as Beckett has already said in Proust, flies in the face of our entire biological nature and is enormously difficult if not absolutely impossible. Nor can we literally call a halt to all our desires, needs and purposes, like we might shut off a water tap.

What else is there, then? We can't avoid projection but we can become aware of it. What we can avoid, therefore, is the naive attachment of word to object. The position developed in The Unnamable is not to reject ordinary thought or try to replace it with some other, more sophisticated metaphysics, but simply to see it for what it is, a form of human projection; neither to encourage nor discourage but passively to allow it to take place without attaching to it any real importance. Similarly, in the Stoic "ablation of desire." We can't stop desire, but we can see through it to a source transcending the individual ego. I experience desires which I act on, but I am not aware of and do not control the ultimate springs of that desire, and this realization alienates the desire from me, blocking the ordinary identification of myself with this desiring ego. In Buddhist thought, from which Beckett borrows heavily, I then begin to identify

155

myself with this underlying source of desire of which the ordinary ego we are aware of is but a manifestation. By becoming aware of projection I continue to have desires and to act on them purposively, but I no longer identify my conscious ego as the ultimate source of the desire. Thus I go through the motions of thought, speech, and action aloof, detached, like the remote onlooker Ionesco speaks of, as in a playful, pointless game. Gradually words and thoughts are thereby detached from their ordinary projective significance, becoming pointless. Thus we still the desire to know, to describe, not by stopping it, but by allowing it to wear itself out, gradually running down like a wound up clock. As talk is exhausted we move toward silence; as the illuminating light of human understanding burns itself out, we anticipate darkness. Thus the goal Becke holds out to us as a real possibility is symbolized by the weightless, evanescent, silent emptiness of absurdity.

What, for example, are we to say about the existence of individual objects? We realize they arise only through the projection of human concerns and interests. But there they are, nonetheless. How should we respond to them? Let them appear, _knowing_ they are human projections.

> And things, what is the correct attitude to adopt toward things? And, to begin with, are they necessary? What a question. But I have few illusions, things are to be expected. The best is not to decide anything...in advance. If a thing turns up, for some reason or another, take it into consideration. Where there are people, it is said, there are things....The thing to avoid...is the spirit of system. People with things, people without things, things without people, what does it matter, I flatter myself it will not take me long to scatter them, whenever I choose to the winds.[26]

As Marie says in several of Ionesco's plays, the important thing is not to take any of this too seriously, tracing out all its connections, pursuing explanations, formulating theories, as though we could finally get to the bottom of things, exhausting reality in the net of our thought. The corollary of this, of course, is that in a detached manner there is no harm in desiring, thinking, speaking, and acting--or even explaining.

156

Beckett's attitude in this passage is also very like the Zen Buddhist attempt to reconcile the proclaimed emptiness of reality with the cluttered world of ordinary sense perception. We are not to pretend the latter doesn't exist, but simply to realize that it is a form of human projection. As the San-lun scholar, Seng-chao wrote in the 5th century,

> When we say that there is neither existence nor non-existence, does it mean to wipe out all the myriad things, blot out our seeing and hearing, and be in a state without sound, form or substance before we can call it truth? Truly, truth is in accord with things as they are and therefore is opposed to none....Not being existent and not being nonexistent do not mean that there are no things, but that all things are not things in the absolute metaphysical sense...Therefore the scripture [of Nagarjuna] says, "Matter is empty by virtue of its own nature; it is not empty because it has been destroyed."[27]

Similarly, in the famous Zen exchange between Wo-luan and Hui-neng, Wo-luan had written,

> I, Wo-luan, know a device
> Whereby to blot out all my thoughts;
> The objective world no more stirs the mind,
> And daily matures my Enlightenment!

To which Hui-neng, Zen's Fifth Patriarch, responded,

> I, Hui-neng, know no device,
> My thoughts are not suppressed.
> The objective world ever stirs the mind,
> And what's the use of maturing Enlightenment?[28]

Similarly, the attempt in the Bhagavad-Gita to reconcile the active life with the illusion of goal-directed activity--simply act without attachment to the object of desire.

As we saw in Proust, despite the extreme relativity of concepts such as the permanent ego or the unchanging object, in order to communicate we must select some of these necessary fictions. In The Unnameable, as in all his important fiction, Beckett selects the point of view of the unchanging subject in a fixed location, looking out upon a world in which objects have completely dissolved and broken down.

> But the best is to think of myself as fixed and at
> the centre of this place, whatever its shape and
> extent may be. This is also probably the most
> pleasing to me. In a word, no change apparently
> since I have been here, disorder of the lights
> perhaps an illusion, all change to be feared,
> incomprehensible uneasiness.[29]

This is the standpoint of Beckett's central characters
in _Endgame_, tied to one spot looking out upon a bleak,
empty world.

> As Berenger says in Ionesco's _A Stroll in the Air_,
> the point is to get away from the _need_ to explain, to
> justify, the intellectual's compulsion to go beyond the
> given trivia of daily life toward the construction of a
> theory which will tie it all together, making more
> sense of it than it really has.

> If I could be a forest, caught in a thicket,
> or wandering around in circles, it would be
> the end of this blither, I'd describe the
> leaves, one by one,...Those are good moments,
> for one who has not to say, but it's not I,
> it's not I, where am I, what am I doing, all
> this time, as if that mattered, but there it
> is, that takes the heart out of you, your
> heart isn't in it any more...it's not love,
> not curiosity, it's because you're tired, you
> want to stop...lie no more, speak no more,
> close your eyes,...after that you'll make
> short work of it.[30]

The main thing to avoid is the "desire to know," the
pretension, that is, of trying to reduce reality to the
form of human thought.

> From the unexceptionable order which has pre-
> vailed here up to date may I infer that such
> will always be the case? I may of course.
> But the mere fact of asking myself such a
> question gives me to reflect....Can it be I
> am prey of a genuine preoccupation, of a need
> to know as one might say?[31]

> Deplorable mania, when something happens, to
> inquire what. If only I were not obliged to
> manifest. And why speak of a cry? Perhaps it

> is something breaking, some two things
> colliding. There are sounds here, from
> time to time, let that suffice.[32]

> Madness, the mad wish to know, to remember...
> I won't be caught at that again...And now let
> us think no more about it, think no more about
> anything, think no more.[33]

At the same time, the goal proposed is a difficult
one, as Becket recognizes. We are caught in the middle,
as Camus also recognized, in the dilemma of being unable
to really understand coupled with an inability to ignore
the bits of partial understanding we do have. We haven't
anything to say, yet we can't be quiet either.

> Yes, in my life, since we must call it so,
> there were three things, the inability to
> speak, the inability to be silent and
> solitude.

The proposed solution, admittedly difficult, is to accept
the world as it appears to us without attaching to it
any absolute importance, to engage in practical action,
as the Bhagavad-Gita suggests, without attachment to the
goal of action, to speak without imagining our words
attached to any independent reality. This, of course,
is difficult. Our very nature is to project a world of
human interests. Even when we realize the absolute
correspondence of word and object is an illusion, the
projected world does not go away. Yet as Berenger affirms
in A Stroll in the Air, behind our ordinary biological
nature there may lie an even deeper instinct to escape
projection, to embrace emptiness, in Berenger's words,
"to fly." As the Buddhists say, perhaps our true nature
is not the ordinary one we are most aware of.

> Impossible to stop them, impossible to stop,
> I'm in words, made of words, others' words,
> ...the air, the walls, the floor, the ceiling,
> all words, the whole world is here with me,
> I'm in the air, the walls,...everything yields,
> opens, ebbs, flows, like flakes, I'm all these
> flakes, meeting, mingling, falling asunder...
> I'm all these words, all these strangers, this
> dust of words, with no ground for their settling
> ...and nothing else, yes, something else, that
> I'm something quite different, a quite different
> thing, a wordless thing in an empty place, a hard
> shut dry cold black place, where nothing stirs,
> nothing speaks.[34]

159

This, then, is the goal of emptiness, however difficult
to attain.

> If I could speak and yet say nothing, really
> nothing...But it seems impossible to speak
> and yet say nothing, you think you have
> succeeded, but you always overlook something,
> a little yes, a little...And yet I do not
> despair, this time...of not going from here,
> of ending here. What prevents the miracle is
> the spirit of method to which I have perhaps
> been a little too addicted.[35]

> I don't mind failing, it's a pleasure, but I
> want to go silent. Not as just now, the better
> to listen, but peacefully, victorious, without
> ulterior object. Then it would be a life worth
> having, a life at last.[36]

As we saw in the second chapter (Camus), so long as
absurdity is perceived privately as the absence of somethi
which ought to be present, whether reason, meaning, knowledge, or whatever, the perception of absurdity is tragic
and heavy. The light side of absurdity consists in
removing the hope, or expectation that the world ought to
be reasonable, meaningful, knowable. If Beckett is silent
ly listening, he is still expecting, hoping, waiting for
an answer, like the characters in Waiting for Godot, and
thus still locked in the illusion of some final and
complete answer. In addition to having an answer and not
having an answer is also the lack of interest in asking
the question, which Beckett seeks.

> Silence, yes, but what silence! For it is
> all very fine to keep silent, but one has
> also to consider the kind of silence one
> keeps. I listened. One might as well
> speak and be done with it.[37]

If, like God, our understanding penetrated to the
heart of reality, there would be no problem. If, like a
stone, we had absolutely no sense of the world, there woul
equally be no problem. The problem is that we are stuck
in a hopeless compromise between the two, illuminating
partial glimpses of the world from interested human points
of view, but unable to know things as they really are in
themselves. This is what prevents complete acceptance of
the empty side of absurdity.

> This meaningless voice which prevents you from
> being nothing, just barely prevents you from
> being nothing and nowhere, just enough to
> keep alight this yellow flame feebly darting

from side to side, panting, as if straining
to tear itself from its wick, it should never
have been lit, or it should never have been fed,
or it should have been put out.[38]

What he wants is to be beyond the desire to know,
neither knowing nor realizing he doesn't know, and not
wanting to know. But this highly desirable goal cannot
be achieved at once, but only after the desire to speak
and to know is thoroughly exhausted, having worn itself
out, as in a Zen koan. As a watch, left to itself,
continues to run, but not indefinitely. Sheer inertia
carries it along for awhile, but hourly slowing down,
it eventually comes to a stop. So habit carries thought,
speech and action along past the recognition of their
illusory goal for a time, eventually wears down, and
stops. As Wittgenstin said at the end of the Tractatus,
we philosophize in order to get rid of philosophizing.
So Becket proposes in The Unnamable to talk his way into
silence.

My speech-parched voice at rest would fill
with spittle, I'd let it flow over and over,
happy at last, dribbling with life, my pensum
ended, in the silence...Squeeze, squeeze, not
too hard, but squeeze a little longer, this
is perhaps about you, and your goal at hand.
After ten thousand words?[39]

As Berenger realized in A Stroll in the Air, the
last illusion for the intellectual is the attempt to
explain the profound limitations of all explanation, to
theorize about the fallibility of theorizing--this, in
short, is the last goal-directed activity we take
seriously. Thus the image in Beckett's plays of the
immobile subject, not going anywhere, not wanting to go
anywhere, which also calls to mind the Buddha's refusal
to leave his fixed place beneath the Bo tree until he
had made an end of his attachments to the ordinary
world.

All this business of a labour to be accomplished,
before I can end, of words to say, a truth to
recover, in order to say it, before I can end,
of an imposed task, once known, long neglected,
finally forgotten, to perform, before I can be
done with speaking, done with listening, I
invented it all, in the hope it would console
me, help me to go on, allow me to think of myself as somewhere on a road, moving, between a
beginning and an end, gaining ground, losing

161

ground,...but somehow making headway. All
lies. I have nothing to do, that is to say
nothing in particular. I have to speak,
whatever that means. Having nothing to
say, no words but the words of others, I
have to speak.[40]

It's of me now I must speak, even if I have
to do it with their language it will be a
start, a step toward silence and the end of
madness, the madness of having to speak and
not being able to, except of things that
don't concern me...that they have crammed me
full to prevent me from saying who I am...
Dear incomprehension, it's thanks to you
I'll be myself, in the end. Nothing will
remain of all the lies they have glutted me
with. And I'll be myself at last, as a
starveling belches his odorless wind, before
the bliss of a coma.[41]

Other images of this blissful emptiness he hopes to
achieve are the Worm, who is truly beyond knowing, and,
unlike Ionesco's recurrent theme of luminosity, the
absolute blackness when the flickering light of conscious
inquiry and projection finally ceases.

Worm, to say he does not know what he is, where
he is, what is happening, is to underestimate
him. What he does not know is that there is
anything to know. His senses tell him nothing,
nothing about himself, nothing about the rest,
and this distinction is beyond him. Feeling
nothing, knowing nothing, he exists nevertheless, but not for himself, for others, others
conceive him and say, Worm is, since we conceive
him...The one ignorant of himself and silent,
ignorant of his silence and silent, who could
not be and gave up trying.[42]

As we saw in our discussion of Aristotle in the first
chapter, although things exist in the world without the
aid of human consciousness, it is only with human thought
and the formulation of "essence" that existence becomes
an issue or concern. Without essence there is no awareness of existence. Outside the orbit of this concern for
and awareness of existence is the ultimate silence Beckett
refers to in an earlier passage above, a silence which
is beyond listening, not even knowing it is silence, a
silence which has transcended the tragic distance between
the desire to speak and the impossibility of saying nothing

162

The other symbol of euphoric emptiness in The Unnamable is total, pitch-black darkness, a recurring image in Beckett's plays, particularly Endgame. In this set of images, light symbolizes ideal, absolute knowledge, the complete correspondence of word and object, thought and reality, the kind of knowledge God has (and which, in Beckett's earlier view, the Idealists have). Darkness is the complete absence of that knowledge which we find in Worm. Both are ideal states, however; as human beings, we are caught in between these two extremes capable of neither completely, yet equally incapable of renouncing either completely. Thus we ordinarily live neither in light nor in darkness, but in "the grey," not knowing but still desiring to know, not saying anything, but unable to keep silent, capable of partial understanding but incapable of total understanding. Just as Beckett's goal is to move from talk we do not take seriously to silence, so we begin in the grey and move toward black- ness. And just as silence will finally be achieved by talking ourselves out, so darkness will come when the dim grey light of projecting understanding finally burns itself out. The lead characters of Beckett's plays are always located in the very last stage of the move from grey to darkness, like Ionesco's characters, though in a different set of images, on the verge of flight, but not able to remain aloft for long.

> Air, the air, is there anything to be squeezed from that old chestnut? Close to me it is grey, dimly transparent, and beyond that charmed circle deepens and spreads its fine impenetrable veils...This grey, first murky, then frankly opaque, is luminous nonetheless.[43]

> Whether all grow black, or all grow bright, or all remain grey, it is grey we need, to begin with, because of what it is, and of what it can do, made of bright and black, unable to shed the former, or the latter, and be the latter or the former alone.[44]

> The grey means nothing, the grey silence is not necessarily a mere lull, to be got through some- how, it may be final, or it may not. But the lamps unattended will not burn on forever, on the contrary, they will go out, little by little, without attendents to charge them anew, and go silent, in the end. Then it will be black. But it is with the black as with the grey, the black proves nothing either, as to the nature of the silence which it inspissates (as it were).[45]

In the grey, looking forward to the black, but not there
yet and perhaps incapable of ever getting there--this is
the posture of most of Beckett's fictional characters,
as we will see. Beckett's final image of the blissful
emptiness, unlike Ionesco's image of bright, luminous
light, is of the immobile, unchanging will-less self
confronting a darkened, empty space.

> There, now there is no one here but me,...
> these creatures have never been, only I and
> this black void have ever been. And the
> sound? No, all is silent. And the lights,
> on which I had set such store, must they too
> go out? Yes, out with them, there is no light
> here. No grey either, black is what I should
> have said. Nothing then but me, of which I
> know nothing, except that I have never uttered,
> and this black, of which I know nothing either,
> except that it is black, and empty.[46]

These themes are very carefully worked out in all
of Beckett's fiction, most successfully in the plays,
but also in his novels, which we will examine first,
though very briefly. These novesl are written in a
Joycean third-person stream-of-consciousness style,
though, unlike The Unnamable, they do have a thin
action plot, dealing with the rather insignificant
adventures of a single socially outcast man, whether
Watt, Murphy or Molloy, from whom the novels take their
titles. These commonplace adventures fairly trans-
parently symbolize the movement of an individual toward
the goal of blissful emptiness, the down-and-out
characters representing someone almost but not quite
having succeeded in transcending the ordinary conventional world of mundane middle-class concerns. Unlike Ionesco
characters who are generally middle-class, educated and
professional, Beckett's characters are out of the mainstre
of ordinary life. Beckett makes much of the irony that
these normally despised creatures are to be envied, not
pitied. Their only problem is that they are not far
enough out of the conventional rut.

Watt (1953), for example, discovers, like Roquentin
in Nausea, the painful absurd detachment of word and
object, the failure of words to attach meaningfully to
their objects.

> For Watt now found himself in the midst of
> things which, if they consented to be named,
> did so as it were with reluctance...Looking
> at a pot, for example,...it was in vain that
> Watt said, Pot, pot. Well, perhaps not quite

in vain, but nearly. For it was not a pot,
the more he looked,...reflected....It
resembled a pot, it was almost a pot, but
it was not a pot of which one could say,
Pot, pot, and be comforted. It was in
vain that it answered, with unexceptionable
adequacy, all the purposes, and performed
all the offices of a pot, it was not a pot
...[It was] painful to Watt...having to do
with things of which the known name...was
not the name, any more for him...For the
pot remained a pot...for everyone but Watt.[47]

   In an earlier novel, Murphy (1938), the central
character attempts to work his way out of this painful
dislocation of word and object, essence and existence.
In this early work Beckett is still thinking his way
through the Idealist program of retreating from the
illusory objective world to a subjective world within.
In the novel this is symbolized by Murphy's positive
attitude toward insanity, envying the schizophrenic's
rejection of the world in favor of a private inner
world.

Murphy's mind pictured itself as a large
hollow sphere, hermetically closed to the
universe without... [but] not an impoverish-
ment...Nothing ever had been, was or would
be in the universe outside it but was already
present...in the universe inside it.[48]

There was the mental fact and there was the
physical fact equally real if not equally
pleasant... Thus Murphy felt himself split
in two, a body and a mind.[49]

   Murphy moves from outer to inner in terms of the
light-dark images of The Unnamable, where light is the
projective tendency of mind to illuminate and thereby
construct a comprehensible interpreted external reality,
while dark is our latent ("virtual") capacity to see
through this illusion, turning it off.

The mind felt its actual part to be above
and bright, its virtual beneath and fading
into dark...There were three zones, light,
half-light, dark, each with its speciality.[50]

The light zone is the ordinary, successful projection of
an existing reality external to us and therefore outside
the control of our will, somewhat like Coleridge's

notion of "primary Imagination."

> In the first were the forms, with parallel,
> radiant abstract of the day's life, with
> elements of physical experience available
> for a new arrangement...Here the whole
> physical fiasco became a howling success.[51]

The second is the world of imagination, in which we freely
reconstitute from elements of ordinary experience pure
essences, released from existence, like the song Roquenti
admires in <u>Nausea</u> and something like Coleridge's "second-
ary Imagination." This is essentially the Schopenhaueria
"aesthetic" stage which Beckett now sees as only intermediary to the more important and final third stage of
darkness. Since these pure objects of thought are no
longer perceived as contrary to our individual wills, the
attitude toward them is, as we saw in Schopenhauer, one
of peaceful contemplation, as Roquentin also found. "In
the second were the forms without parallel. Here the
pleasure was contemplative."[52]

In the third zone, the dark, we neither naively
project a world nor deliberately construct an imaginary
one, we simply become <u>aware</u> of projection. Part of this
awareness is the realization of the limits of the self-
contained power and freedom of the conscious ego. We
are free, of course, to act upon our desires and concerns
as they present themselves to us, but we do not control
these desires themselves. They are deeply rooted in our
biological nature. An important part of the awareness
of projection, therefore, is the recognition that the
self-subsistent ego freely acting to possess or avoid
self-subsistent objective entities is itself a part, inde
the core of projection, and hence, an illusion. Reality
must not, therefore, be equated or confused with it, sinc
reality transcends this human way of thinking. Thus in
the dark zone, as Schopenhauer suggests, objective
distinctions and subjective distinctions both collapse,
including the primary subject-object distinction, into a
mystical will-less identification with a transcendent
reality. To compound the comparison, the final release
of will acts as a new kind of freedom, an ironic freedom
<u>from</u> the individual freedom of the will.

> The third, the dark, was a flux of forms, a
> perpetual coming together and a falling
> asunder of forms...[A] sensation of being a
> missile without phenomena or target, caught
> up in a tumult of non-Newtonian motion...
> as his body set him free more and more in

his absolute mind...in the will-lessness, a
mote in its absolute freedom.[53]

For Murphy, who works in a mental institution, the
dark zone, to which he aspires, is exemplified in the
schizophrenic rejection of reality in favor of the
cultivation of some private fantasy. Like the
Shakespearean fool, Murphy reverses our usual assessment
of madness. The insane are less mad than the madness of
normal existence which Beckett describes in The Unnamable.
Murphy begins to realize that psychiatric treatment
merely

> translates the sufferer from his own pernicious
> little private dungheap to the glorious world
> of discrete particulars..to wonder, love, hate,
> desire, rejoice and howl in a reasonable
> balanced manner...with the society of others
> in the same predicament...All this was duly
> revolting to Murphy, whose experience as a
> physical and rational being obliged him to call
> sanctuary what the psychiatrists called exile
> and to think of the patients not as banished
> from a system of benefits but as escaped from
> a colossal fiasco.[54]

It is not this dark zone of blissful emptiness which
Murphy seeks, "I am not of the big world, I am of the
little world," and which he achieves just as he is dying.

> Murphy began to see nothing, that colorlessness
> which is such a rare post-natal treat, being
> the absence...not of percipere but of percipi.
> His other senses also found themselves at peace,
> an unexpected pleasure. Not the numb peace of
> their own suspension, but the positive peace
> that comes when the somethings give way, or
> perhaps simply add up, to the Nothing, than
> which in the guffaw of the Abderite naught is
> more real. Time did not cease, that would be
> asking too much, but the wheels of rounds and
> pauses did, as Murphy...continued to suck in,
> through all the posterns of his withered soul,
> the accidentless One-and-Only, conveniently
> called Nothing.[55]

The Abderite referred to is the Greek stoic, Democritus
of the Abdera, who said, as Beckett is fond of quoting,
"Nothing is more real than nothing." There are also
obvious references to Buddhist thought, not only in the
notion of reality as "the Nothing" (rather than the all-

167

encompassing monistic reality whether of the Brahmins or of the Idealists), but also in the reference to time as "the wheels of rounds and pauses." It is not clear whic of the Buddhist authors Beckett consulted, though it is clear that he did read some translations of Buddhist tex as did Ionesco. Nonetheless, it might be interesting to compare Murphy's final statement above with the Zen patriarch, Huang-po's explanation of "the Void" as a symbol of the transcendence of reality from all human categories.

> [Reality] is not green nor yellow and has
> neither form nor appearance. It does not
> belong to the categories of things which
> exist or do not exist...It is neither long
> nor short, for it transcends all limits,
> measures, names, traces and comparisons.
> It is that which you see before you--begin
> to reason about it and you at once fall
> into error. It is like the boundless
> void which cannot be fathomed or measured.[56]

Molloy (1966) also describes the attempt to escape the projected world in which we have imprisoned ourselve into a blissful emptiness beyond names, explanations, structures of thought.

> For to know is nothing, not to want to know
> anything likewise, but to be beyond knowing
> anything, that is when peace enters in, to
> the soul of the incurious seeker.[58]

> Not to want to say, not to know what you
> want to say, not to be able to say what you
> think you want to say, and never to stop
> saying, or hardly ever, that is the thing
> to keep in mind, even in the heat of
> composition.[59]

> And even my sense of identity was wrapped in
> a namelessness often hard to penetrate, as
> we have seen I think. And so on for all the
> other things which made merry with my senses...
> There could be no things but nameless things,
> no names but thingless names...What do I
> know now...when the icy words hail down upon
> me, the icy meanings, and the world dies too,
> foully named. All I know is what the words
> know, and the dead things, and that makes a
> handsome little sum, with a beginning, a middle
> and an end as in the well-built phrase...it

little matters what I say...Saying is inventing.
Wrong...You invent nothing, you think you are
inventing.[60]

There were times when I forgot not only who I
was, but that I was, forgot to be, then I was
no longer that sealed jar to which I owed my
being so well preserved, but a wall gave way
and I filled with roots and tame stems..But
that did not happen to me often, mostly I
stayed in my jar...But in there you have to
be careful, ask yourself questions. For my
part I willingly asked myself questions, one
after the other...And yet it meant nothing
to me to be still there.[61]

In the novels Beckett's characters describe their
plight in terms of such images as darkness, silence,
sealed enclosures, and a journey. In the plays Beckett
displays these images concretely, and as in Ionesco's
plays, the characters do the things Watt, Murphy and
Molloy talk about. Therefore the plays provide Beckett's
most successful exploration of such themes, especially
Waiting for Godot and Endgame, which we will examine in
some detail.

Waiting for Godot deals with the problem of cutting
the last links that bind us to the projected world of
human purposes and interests. The central characters
in this play, Vladimir and Estragon, find themselves in
the difficult intermediary position Beckett defines in
The Unnamable, unable to say anything and yet also unable
to keep silent. They find themselves already on the
outer fringes of the conventionally constructed world,
past their prime of life, socially outcast or at least
insignificant, but not quite able to take that final step.
They don't take it seriously any more, but they can't
quite give up the game entirely. They have succeeded in
penetrating the naive illusion of projection, and no
longer attach any real significance to their speech or
action. Yet they cling half-heartedly to one final
illusion, the hope that Godot will come.

The central dramatic problem of the play is not,
then, whether Godot will come or not, but whether to
continue waiting for Godot. The problem is, as we have
seen, Beckett's problem whether we can give it up entirely.

As with most absurdist fiction, the plot is very thin,
Vladimir and Estragon wait each day for Godot with whom
they believe they have an appointment to discuss some

169

possible employment. But by nightfall Godot has not
arrived and Vladimir and Estragon debate whether to retu
the next day to continue their vigil, which, reluctantly
they finally decide to do. But Godot does not arrive
the following day, and so it goes day after day. There
is never much hope of Godot's arriving. They are not
sure there is a Godot, whether he knows them, or even
intended to meet with them, and if he did, it is still
not clear what time of day or even on what day the
appointment was supposed to take place. Still, they are
held to their expectation by the thinnest possible
diminishing thread. Not really expecting him to come,
they can't quite give up the pretense or habit of hoping
he will.

Like most great art Beckett's images are rich in
multiple, overlapping nuances. The tree, for example,
where Vladimir and Estragon wait. Is this the "tree of
life" which is dying, the Bo tree where the Buddha waite
for enlightenment, or the tree of Golgotha? It is not
identical with any of these, of course, but all three
meanings are probably meant to enrich this image.
Certainly Beckett does not discourage any of them.
Vladimir and Estragon, for example, talk about hanging
themselves from the tree, they discuss the happenstance
that one of the two criminals hung with Christ was saved
while the other was not. The name Godot has often been
interpreted as a misspelling of God, all of which
supports and reinforces this religious interpretation.
Godot appears to represent man's thirst for absolute
knowledge; in so far as God is a symbol for the absolute
'Godot' carries this religious connotation. The tree
also symbolizes life, the tree of life, as when the
characters discuss whether it is losing its leaves. But
these nuances of meaning do not support the overall
structure of the play. As with Ionesco, the dominant
thrust of the play is metaphysical; other layers of
meaning, and there are many, are subsidary and supportiv

The two characters, Vladimir and Estragon, represen
the two sides of the problem, the two poles within an
individual which makes final release into blissful empti
ness difficult. Estragon wants to give up waiting,
Vladimir prefers to wait. Each time Estragon proposes
they leave ("I'm going") Vladimir talks him into staying
a little longer. Thus the two characters represent
opposed, but complementary character traits, neither of
which can exist without the other. Vladimir is practica
persistent, a man of fixed habits and little humor, a
literalist who hates dreams and relies on past regulari-

170

ties. Estragon, on the other hand, is a volative, humor-
ous dreamer, a poet who has little faith in theories or
regularities of any sort. Together they represent the
theme of wanting to leave but being unable to do so.

Equally complementary are the other two characters
in the play, Pozzo and Lucky, who appear briefly from
time to time. Pozzo and Lucky represent the folly of
ordinary naive absorption in the world which brings them
nothing but suffering, infirmity, old age and death, as
in traditional Buddhism. Like Ionesco, Beckett supports
his image of absurd heaviness with themes of human brutality, vanity, blind rage and stupidity, with Pozzo and
Lucky standing to one another not only in the mind-body
relation but also in the master-slave relationship. While
Vladimir and Estragon are already on the outer periphery
of naive absorption in the projected world, Pozzo and
Lucky are caught in the center of that illusion. While
Vladimir and Estragon represent an advanced but not final
stage toward complete release, Pozzo and Lucky are still
at an elementary, primitive stage of human awareness.

Involved in the idea of waiting is Beckett's notion,
borrowed from Schopenhauer, of the illusion of purposeful
action through time which we saw earlier in his analysis
of Proust. The ordinary meaningful structure of the
world, as we saw, is based largely on our purposeful
posture toward things, doing something today for the sake
of something else in the future. Thus we connect objects
in the past, present and future into a coherent unity
which ordinarily gives our lives meaning. Thus we manage
to stretch out our lives in pursuing and accomplishing
our life goals. This gives each person's life a
structural development or "story-line", and gives each
of us a sense of meaningfully filled time. But if that
is an illusion, as Beckett believes, the entire facade
of that projected world collapses. Past, present,
future are no longer connected and time becomes something
merely to be spent, filled, gotten through somehow.
Nothing is "accomplished" in time but old age and death,
toward which we have nothing to do but wait.

This is vividly conveyed in Waiting for Godot where
the ordinary span of time bridging past and future
collapses, levelling and shortening everything in its
path. We ordinarily "stretch" out our lives with the
accomplishment of our purposes. Without purpose, time
"snaps back" to something short in significance, though
paradoxically long in boredom. We can see this in
everyday life. When we are bored, with "nothing to do",

171

time drags by endlessly, but when someone asks us later
what we've been doing, we say, "oh, nothing," which is
precisely all we will remember of it later. On the othe
hand, when we are deeply engrossed in some meaningful
pursuit, the hours fly by and we remember it as a full
day packed with accomplishment, and this stretches a day
 which   in another sense was so short. The most common
experience in daily life of time hanging heavily is
waiting for someone, which makes this such a powerful
image in the play.

     Thus Estragon and Vladimir aimlessly wait, passing
time, idling away the hours under a fragile illusion,
which they are barely able to maintain, of meaningful
expectation. This is no reason for living, but only an
excuse. Since nothing significant ever happens, meaning
ful change is an illusion. As Borges points out in his
article on time, without the possibility of purposeful
action the sense of time contracts and there is no more
significance (i.e., "essence") to the span of 80 years
than there is to 80 seconds. Just as objects can be
existentially heavy and essentially light, so time can b
physically long and experientially short. Indeed it is
so short it is reduced to nothing, "shortness" being a
metaphor for the unreality of time. Hence the sense of
a person stretching out his life with activity and
accomplishment is an illusion; he is dead, or as good as
dead, as soon as he is born. As Pozzo says,

     Have you not done tormenting me with your
     accursed time?...One day, is that not
     enough for you, one day like any other
     day he went dumb, one day I went blind,
     one day we'll die, the same day, same
     second...They gave birth astride of a
     grave. The light gleams an instant, then
     it's night once more.

     In this absurdist vision of time, the only thing we
can expect time to bring is death, symbolized in the pla
by nightfall. Each time Pozzo and Lucky appear they hav
become progressively infirm, decrepit, nearer and nearer
to death, although from the standpoint of the absurd
unreality of time, Estragon denies that they have change
But aside from death, time brings nothing, nothing really
ever happens. The opening lines of the play tell the
whole story.

     Estragon: Nothing to be done.
     Vladimir: I'm beginning to come round to that
                opinion.

172

Since the time must be got through somehow they engage in
idle chatter, word games to while away the hours. There
is nothing to do but wait. Or at least this is the most
they can do; the question remains whether they can stop
waiting. Vladimir would like to quit wasting time with
idle talk and get on with some meaningful activity.

> Vladimir: Let's not waste our time in idle
>   discourse! Let us do something,
>   while we have the chance.

This is like Marguerite's position in Exit the King, to
cling to the world of civic duty and significant action.
Estragon, on the other hand, following Marie's advice
as it were, would like to stop talking altogether, to go
silent, as Beckett proposes in The Unnamable.

> Estragon: Let's stop talking for a minute...
>   Why will you never let me sleep.

In the meantime, they agree to pass the hours in
mindless conversation, in a playful parody of meaningful
discourse. The point of talk is gone; all that remains
is the habit of talking, going through the motions, as we
idly go through a routine game to pass the time. Here
Beckett returns to the image in The Unnamable of achieving
silence by talking ourselves out.

> Estragon: In the meantime let us try and
>   converse calmly, since we are
>   incapable of keeping silent.
> Vladimir: You're right, we're inexhaustible.
> Estragon: It's so we won't think.

After Pozzo and Lucky leave Vladimir says,

> Vladimir: That passed the time.
> Estragon: It would have passed in any case.
> Vladimir: Yes, but not so rapidly.

They play a variety of such games, usually at Vladimir's
invitation.

> Estragon: I'm going.
> Vladimir: Will you not play?

This momentarily helps to pass the time and support the
fragile illusion of a normal life in a naively meaningful
world. In the farcial exchange over the boots, Estragon
says to Vladimir, whose nickname is Didi,

                Estragon: We always find something, eh Didi,
                           to give us the impression we exist?

But not for long. In another similar exchange over the
turnips and carrots,

                Vladimir: This is becoming really insignificant.
                Estragon: Not enough.

        Talk, even the most aimless chatter can exhaust the
need to talk, but it can also restore the habitual link
to the ordinary world of conventional concerns, keeping
alive, though faintly, what Beckett calls Habit. Thus b
talking we continue the ordinary madness which prevents
our escape.

                Vladimir: All I know is that the hours are long,
                           under these conditions, and constrains
                           us to beguile them with proceedings
                           which - how shall I say - which may at
                           first sight seem reasonable, until they
                           become a habit. You may say it is to
                           prevent our reason from foundering. No
                           doubt. But has it not long been strayin
                           in the night without end of the abyssal
                           depths?...
                Estragon: We are born mad. Some remain so.

This is the theme of reverse madness we have seen in The
Unnamable and in Murphy.

        Thus, waiting for Godot represents the last remaini
link to the comforting ordinary world of conventional
expectations.

                Estragon (his mouth full of carrot): We're not tie
                Vladimir: I don't hear a word you're saying.
                Estragon (chews, swallows): I'm asking you if we'r
                           tied.
                Vladimir: Tied?
                Estragon: ti-ed.
                Vladimir: How do you mean tied?
                Estragon: Down.
                Vladimir: But to whom? By whom?
                Estargon: To your man.
                Vladimir: To Godot? Tied to Godot! What an idea!
                           No question of it.
                (Pause) For the moment.
                Estragon: His name is Godot?
                Vladimir: I think so.
                Estragon: Fancy that.

                                174

At times it seems best to cling to this thinnest of hopes, despite Estragon's scepticism and reluctance, and so they continue to "squeeze" out more "dead words," clichés, as in Ionesco's The Bald Soprano.

> Estragon: So long as one knows.
> Vladimir: One can bide one's time.
> Estragon: One knows what to expect.
> Vladimir: No further need to worry.
> Estragon: Simply wait.
> Vladimir: We're used to it.

On the other hand, the expectation is a transparent sham which Estragon especially detests.

> Estragon: In the meantime nothing happens...
> Nothing happens, nobody comes, nobody
> goes, it's awful!

Vladimir and Estragon are like two sides of a single person. The dilemma they face requires both these points of view: stubbornly hoping and giving up all hope. Since the presence of the other is a constant reminder of that dilemma, each would be happier without the other, yet they can't exist apart from one another.

> Vladimir (who has been alone): All day I've
> felt in great form...I missed you...
> and at the same time I was happy.
> Estragon: You feel worse when I'm with you.
> I feel better alone too.
> Vladimir: Then why do you always come crawling
> back?
> Estragon: I don't know.

Thus the two exist in a delicate tension. Each prevents the other from his own resolution, Estragon preventing Vladimir from slipping mindlessly back into Habit and Vladimir preventing Estragon from slipping quietly off into silence.

Sometimes, as in an earlier passage, Vladimir seems momentarily to convince Estragon that they are right to wait. At other times Estragon gains the upper hand and Vladimir seems on the verge of giving up the futile waiting. At one point Vladimir continues Pozzo's reflection on the absurd shortness, or rather unreality, of temporal extension, arriving finally almost at Estragon's total rejection of habit and purposeful expectation.

> Vladimir: Astride of a grave and a difficult

birth. Down in the hole, lingeringly,
the grave-digger puts on the forceps.
We have time to grow old. The air is
full of our cries. But habit is a
great deadener...I can't go on.

But at that very moment a young boy appears with a
message from Godot, and Vladimir, his hopes again revived,
agrees to return the following day to wait for Godot.
Estragon, who would rather stop hoping than to have Godot
come, is obviously upset over the boy's appearance.

Estragon: I'm unhappy.

For it looks like Estragon's inseparable partner, Vladimir
will never stop waiting till he dies, that is, until night
fall when they can leave. As Vladimir says earlier to
Pozzo,

Vladimir: Will night ever come?
Pozzo: You don't feel like going until it does?

From Estragon's point of view the more they wait the
more they are drawn into the illusion of Habit, which
Vladimir, however, finds a comfort. About the carrot,
Estragon says,

Estragon: The more you eat the worse it gets.
Vladimir: With me it's the opposite.

Thus the central dilemma is unresolved in Waiting for
Godot. Godot will never come; they would like to but are
unable to stop wanting him to come. They are unable to
take that last step to the wisdom of Worm which Murphy and
Molloy do seem to achieve, if only momentarily. The play
remains, however, a powerful statement of this basic human
dilemma.

The same dilemma motivates another of Beckett's plays
Endgame. The central issue in this play is contained in
the title, the game of bringing our attachment to the worl
to a complete and final end, which in the play is symboliz
by Clov's desire to leave his tyrannical master, Hamm.
Like Vladimir and Estragon, Clov and Hamm represent the
duality of human nature. Hamm, like Vladimir, clings to
the dwindling world he knows and is familiar with, though
more selfishly, possesively than Vladimir (incorporating,
in other words, more of the element of Pozzo). Clov, on
the other hand, resembles Estragon in trying to abandon
this world completely. But, like Vladimir and Estragon,
each needs the other and so, as in Waiting for Godot, the

176

dilemma of Endgame remains unresolved. If Clov leaves,
both he and Hamm will die, Clov, since Hamm has selfishly
hoarded the entire world's supply of food and Hamm because
he depends so heavily on Clov. But so long as Clove remains
he will be stifled by Hamm, eventually becoming another
Hamm. The other pair in the play, Nagg and Nell, Hamm's
ancient and decrepit prents, resemble Lucky and Pozzo's
ridiculous attachment to the ordinary humanly projected
world. Unlike Ionesco's correlative authority figures,
policemen, firemen, etc., the characters in Beckett's plays
who represent the drag of conventionality do not have such
great power over the central characters trying to escape.
The difficulty of ending comes from within the central
characters themselves, and the statement of the problem is
more internal than social.

     Like Ionesco's Exit the King, the play is about ending,
finishing. Will Clov leave or will he remain, eventually
to take Hamm's place? As in Exit the King, some vague
disaster has occurred; everything has been destroyed except
the four characters who live inside a remote walled fortress
or lighthouse. As in Ionesco's The Chairs, this seems to
represent our self-imprisonment within our own minds--the
"large hollow sphere" in Murphy, the "sealed jar" Molloy
tried to break out of, and finally does ("a wall...gave
way"). Hamm can't leave; he is blind and paralyzed (again
like Pozzo) and has to be waited on hand and foot by Clov.
In this respect Clov resembles the slavish attachment of
Lucky to Pozzo in the first act of Waiting for Godot.
Clov moves Hamm around in his chair, brings him what he
needs and takes periodic looks at what is left of the
world outside.

     Hamm represents all the ugly, selfish, egotistical,
possessive attachments which tie us to the world. The
problem is how to end this nagging, unpleasant attachment.
The tone of the play is established in the opening lines.

          Clov: Finished, it's finished, nearly finished,
                 it must be nearly finished.

The most irritating feature of Hamm is his endless stream
of repetitious, trivial questions, symbolizing here, as
in The Unnamable, and Murphy, the illusion that by constant
inquiry we can achieve absolute knowledge.

          Clove: All life long the same question, the
                  same answers.

Hamm is of another opinion.

                         177

Hamm: I love the old questions. Ah, the
        old questions, the old answers.

Inside the fortress, then, is human consciousness,
distinguishing, questioning, constructing. Outside is
nothing, a "grey light" fading into darkenss, as in The
Unnamable. For Hamm, as for Vladimir, the nothingness
outside is simply his death, those forces which will
eventually annihilate his conscious ego, destroying his
carefully constructed fortress. For Clov, it is a means
of escape which can be consciously chosen.

Hamm: Outside of here it's death.
Clov: There's no more nature...In the vicinity
        ...Zero.
Hamm: Nothing stirs.
Clov: The light is sunk...All gone...Gray.
        Gray! Gray!

Hamm, too, realizes it is "finished" but unlike Clov he
resists it, retreating from it, closing himself off from
it within this own mind, and like Camus and Sartre, opposing
his actively questioning consciousness to the nothingness
of the world, which Clov would willingly embrace. Eventual
Hamm will join the nothing outside when, against his will,
he finally dies, but in the meantime he revels in the
opposition of his projecting mind to an alien reality, his
"essence" against the world's "existence."

Hamm: It's finished, we're finished. Nearly
        finished. There'll be no more speech.
Clov: I love order. It's my dream. A world
        where all would be silent and still and
        each thing it its last place, under the
        last dust.
Hamm: It will be the end and there I'll be in
        the old shelter, alone against the silence
        and the stillness. I can hold my peace,
        and sit quiet, it will be all over with
        sound, and motion, all over and done with.

There is no question but that the world is absurd. Reality
transcends completely all the meaning, structure and
essence human beings try to impose on it. The only
question is what attitude to take toward it--heroically
defying it like Camus or embracing it like Berenger in
Ionesco's later plays.

Hamm and Clov both see it ending, though in different
ways. One is simply to know it is an illusion, defying it

178

and waiting for death to end it for us. This is Hamm's position, "Outside of here it's death." Thus Hamm screams at his parents for their desperate clinging to life from their filthy trash cans despite the loss of arms, legs and various senses.

> Hamm: Have you not finished? Will you never
>   finish? Will this never finish?

Like Pozzo, Hamm waits for death, just as Vladimir waits for night to end it for him by ending his life.

> Hamm: One day you'll be blind, like me. You'll
>   be sitting there, a speck in the void,
>   in the dark, forever, like me...Infinite
>   emptiness will be all around you...and
>   there you'll be like a little bit of grit
>   in the middle of the steppe.

The other possibility which Clov, and presumably Beckett himself, seeks is willingly to embrace nothingness, releasing the ego from its distinction from and opposition to the world. At one point it looks as though Clov will leave, but then he sees a young boy outside. Like the young boy sent by Godot, this raises the faint possibility that all is not dead and empty, which depresses Clov, as the appearance of the boy depresses Estragon, with the thought that once again Habit's old illusions have received fresh blood and could continue indefinitely.

> Clov (looking at earth for last time): Nothing...
>   nothing...good...good...nothing...good. Bad
>   luck to it!...(dismayed) Looks like a small
>   boy.

Later Clov again voices his goal of willingly embracing the empty silence beyond his selfish ego.

> Clov: Then one day, suddenly, it ends,...I
>   ask the words that remain...They have
>   nothing to say. I open the door of my
>   cell and go...I say to myself that the
>   earth is extinguished though I never saw
>   it lit. It's easy going. When I fall
>   I'll weep for happiness.

But as the curtain falls Clov stand with one hand on the door looking back at Hamm and the audience is left wondering whether he finally leaves or whether this is simply one more among many futile attempts to leave, part of

179

a "game" they play, over and over again, of "ending."

The one play in which the attachment to the projected world is finally achieved is the mime, Act without Words, which Beckett wrote to follow Endgame. In the mime a lone man is flung out onto a "dazzling light" "desert." He is drawn by whistles in various directions; objects tempt him, including water, but as he reaches for them they retreat just beyond his grasp. Finally, the character overcomes any desire for the objects and makes no attempt to reach out for them even when they are dangled immediate in front of him. In the end he remains immobile, like the Buddha under the Bo tree, refusing to move--Beckett's goal of joyous, empty silence finally achieved.

Chapter Five: References

1. Samuel Beckett, _Proust_ (New York: Grove Press, 1931), pp. 7-8.

2. _Ibid._, p. 47.

3. _Ibid._, p. 16.

4. _Ibid._, p. 12-13.

5. _Ibid._, pp. 26-27.

6. _Ibid._, p. 10.

7. _Ibid._, p. 11.

8. _Ibid._, pp. 6-7.

9. _Ibid._, p. 41.

10. _Ibid._, p. 3.

11. _Ibid._, p. 7.

12. _Ibid._, p. 46.

13. Samuel T. Coleridge, letter to Sotheby, 1802, in _Biographia Literaria_, J. Shawcross, ed., v. 1 (London: Oxford University Press, 1962), p. xxxiv.

14. Coleridge, _Miscellaneous Criticism._

15. Nietzsche, in Erich Heller, _The Artist's Journey into the Interior_ (London: Secker and Warburg, 1966), p. 103.

16. D.H. Lawrence ,_Apocalypse._

17. Baudelaire, in Heinz Werner, _Comparative Psychology of Mental Development_ (Chicago: Follet, 1948), p. 82.

18. Beckett, _op. cit._, pp. 55-56.

19. _Ibid._, p. 56.

20. _Ibid._, p. 57.

21. G.W.F. Hegel, _The Philosophy of Fine Art_, F.P.B. Osmaston, trans., v. 2 (London: G. Bell and Sons, 1920), p. 295.

22. _Ibid._

23. Heinrich Heine, in Heller, _op. cit._

24. Nagarjuna, _Madhyamika Shastra_, quoted by Chi-tsang from the Chinese translation, _The Chung Lun_, in _A Source Book in Chinese Philosophy_, Wing-tsit, trans. and ed. (Princeton: Princeton University Press, 1963), p. 3

25. _Ibid._, in Heinrich Zimmer, _Philosophies of Indi_ (New York: Meridian Books, 1957), p. 521.

26. Beckett, _The Unnamable_, author, trans. (New Yor Grove Press, 1958), pp. 4-5.

27. Seng-chao, "The Emptiness of the Unreal," in _A Source Book in Chinese Philosophy_, _op. cit._, p. 353.

28. Hui-neng, in _ibid._

29. Beckett, _op. cit._, p. 9.

30. _Ibid._, p. 158.

31. _Ibid._, p. 8.

32. _Ibid._, p. 10.

33. _Ibid._, p. 68.

34. _Ibid._, p. 139.

35. _Ibid._, p. 20.

36. _Ibid._, p. 30.

37. _Ibid._, p. 28.

38. _Ibid._, pp. 116-117.

39. _Ibid._, p. 30.

40, _Ibid._, pp. 35-36; cf. Huang-po, _op. cit._, "'Study the Way' is just a figure of speech...You must not allow this name ('Way') to lead you into forming a mental conce of a road," a statement which might well have been utter by Wittgenstein.

41. Beckett, _op. cit._, p. 51.

42. _Ibid._, pp. 82-83.

43. Ibid., p. 16.

44. Ibid., p. 17.

45. Ibid., p. 109.

46. Ibid., p. 21.

47. Beckett, Watt (London: John Calder (Juniper Books), 1963 (Olympia, 1953)), pp. 78-79.

48. Beckett, Murphy (New York: Grove Press, 1957 (1938)), pp. 107-108.

49. Ibid., pp. 108-109.

50. Ibid., pp. 109-111.

51. Ibid., p. 111.

52. Ibid.

53. Ibid., pp. 112-113.

54. Ibid., pp. 177-178.

55. Ibid., p. 246.

56. Huang-po, The Teaching of Huang-Po, John Blofeld, trans. (New York: Grove Press, 1959), p. 29.

57. Ibid., pp. 122-123.

58. Beckett, Molloy (London: Calder and Boyars (Juniper Books)), 1966, p. 68.

59. Ibid., p. 29.

60. Ibid., p. 33.

61. Ibid., pp. 51-52; cf. the "sealed jar" with the "large hollow sphere" in Murphy.

RITTER LIBRARY
BALDWIN-WALLACE COLLEGE

ABOUT THE AUTHOR

H. Gene Blocker is Professor of Philosophy at Ohio University. Educated at the University of Chicago (B.A., 1960), and the University of California, Berkeley (Ph.D., 1966), Professor Blocker has taught philosophy of art and literature at the University of Aberdeen, Scotland, and the University of Sierra Leone, West Africa. In addition to numerous publications in scholarly periodicals, Dr. Blocker has published several books, including Philosophy of Art (Scribner's, 1979), John Rawls' Theory of Social Justice (co-editor, Ohio University Press, 1979), The Meaning of Meaninglessness (Martinus Nijhoff, 1974), and Introduction to Philosophy (co-author, Van Nostrand, 1974). Gene Blocker is also an avid collector of African and Precolumbian art and plays cornet in a traditional jazz band.

3673

DATE DUE

APR 27 1983
MAY 9 1988

MAY 21 1988

WITHDRAWN

DEMCO 38-297